THE
ALEXANDER
TECHNIQUE

THE
ALEXANDER
TECHNIQUE

Wilfred Barlow

WARNER BOOKS

A Warner Communications Company

WARNER BOOKS EDITION

This Warner Books Edition is published by
arrangement with Alfred A. Knopf, Inc.
Photographs by Wilfred Barlow
Warner Books, Inc., 75 Rockefeller Plaza, New York,
N. Y. 10019

A Warner Communications Company

Printed in the United States of America
First Printing, April 1980
10 9 8 7 6 5 4 3 2 1

Library of Congress Cataloging in Publication Data
Barlow, Wilfred.   The Alexander technique.
"Originally published in Great Britain in a slightly
different form under title: *The Alexander principle.*"
Reprint of the ed. published by Knopf, New York.
Includes bibliographical references.
1. Alexander technique. I. Title.
[BF172.B37   1980]   616.8'913   79-18975
ISBN 0-446-97280-0

CONTENTS

PART I—PRINCIPLES

1. *The Alexander Principle*   3
2. *Use and Mis-use*   15
3. *Balance and Rest*   56
4. *Use and Disease*   92
5. *Mental Health*   125
6. *The Psycho-Mechanics of Sex*   142

PART II—PRACTICE

7. *Teaching the Principle*   167
8. *Learning the Principle*   185
9. *Applying the Principle*   200

Source Notes   217
References   219
Index   follows page 221

Part I

PRINCIPLES

CHAPTER 1

The Alexander Principle

The Alexander Principle is a hypothesis: it is not an established, absolute truth, but a new way of looking at things,
a new way of organizing oneself. In time, it may be proved
to be false, but it could prove to be one of the most important evolutionary hypotheses that human beings have ever
devised for themselves.

The Principle proposes a different way of living and of
seeing one's life, not different in the sense of making its
users into oddities, but different in that its users can learn
to adopt other criteria for themselves and for the people
they live with. Its users (over the thirty years I have observed it) seem to be able to adapt more successfully than
most people in their social, artistic, and biological spheres.
And, most important of all, they appear to live longer and
more healthily.

The Alexander Principle states: that there are certain

ways of using your body which are better than certain other ways; that when you reject these better ways of using your body, your functioning will begin to suffer in some important respects; that it is useful to assess other people by the way they use themselves.

This approach is not a fringe medicine, a neo-progressive education, a religious escape, or a quack science. It is a difficult, controlled approach to living that leads, through a discipline, to personal freedom and health which are possible to some extent for most people at most ages.

The Alexander Principle sounds at first deceptively simple. I have called it the Alexander Principle because, as far as I know, Matthias Alexander was the first person to state it, and I have endeavored in this book to give an account of it that will be helpful to someone who has never heard of him.

As for Alexander himself, he was born in 1869 in rural Australia. To judge by his reviews, he was a successful young Shakespearean actor in Sydney until he was increasingly plagued by voice trouble. In the nineteenth century, little was known of speech training or speech therapy as we now know it, and Alexander's recurrent loss of voice brought his stage career to an untimely close.

In desperation, and with little medical or physiological knowledge, he decided that by use of a mirror he must carefully examine the way he was using his muscles when he spoke. It is a common observation that when people speak they are likely to carry out quite inappropriate movements through the whole of their bodies. A glance at a television screen often shows announcers and commentators who have persistent mannerisms when they speak. Alexander was particularly struck by curious movements that took place around his neck and head as he spoke. Although the types of curious movement that can take place in this region are numerous, he picked out the most prevalent one, which consists of tightening the head backward on the neck and downward into the chest. At this point—and indeed for the remainder of his life—he became concerned with the types of muscular usage that arise when people react to a stimulus. He was in fact a child of his times, with its stimulus-response psychology and the behaviorism that Pavlov and his dogs helped to foster. Fortunately, Alexander's initial observations provided enough impetus to enable him to develop and refine his methods until the end of his days.

I knew Alexander intimately for more than a decade, married into his family, and have edited the *Alexander Journal* for many years. In his later years, he asked my wife and me to be responsible for the future of his work, and at his request I founded the Alexander Society of Teachers with this in view. I know as well as anyone his personal idiosyncrasies—they wear extremely well now that he is dead, however much they may have upset people in his lifetime. I suspect that if Alexander were alive today he would be speaking of our present condition. His predictions of our present personal and social unhappinesses have come about very much as he foretold.

I should perhaps briefly mention the contact that I had with him and his ideas before and after World War II. He had come to London in 1904, aged 34, from Sydney, where he had been the director of the Sydney Dramatic and Operatic Conservatorium. His concept of USE was not very clearly formulated at that time, but between 1904 and 1955 he published four books, of which the shortest and perhaps most to the point was *The Use of the Self* (1932). This book led to considerable interest on the part of doctors and teachers and many others, especially in the 1930s. Among his pupils, for example, were George Bernard Shaw, Aldous

Huxley, Stafford Cripps, and Archbishop William Temple.

I first heard of Alexander through reading Aldous Huxley's *Ends and Means* in 1937. It took some time to get to him, but after three months of persistent badgering I eventually managed to meet him. Almost everything he said made sense to me, and I decided to study under him to learn how to teach his methods. We became very close friends and he certificated me as a teacher in 1940, just after the outbreak of war. Working in wartime London became difficult and he was evacuated, with his school, to America in the summer of 1940.

His time in the United States, from 1940 to 1943, was not a very happy one for him. He wrote to me frequently, increasingly distressed by the turn the war was taking. It looked at that time as though his work and his Principle could easily become lost—nearly all his teachers were in the armed forces. I myself spent a boring few years as a regimental medical officer, seeing little either of the enemy or of medicine. It did, however, give me the opportunity to carry out research on large groups of young men and women who were under great emotional and physical stress, and in the process to confirm many of Alexander's observations on USE.

Eventually, Alexander could bear the separation from England no longer, and he returned to London in the summer of 1943. He was now an old man and was becoming embittered by the refusal of the medical and educational establishment to recognize his ideas. The very qualities that had led him to his scientific discoveries—single-mindedness and questioning—tended now toward suspiciousness. This was not helped by an outrageous attack on his work in South Africa, which culminated in a libel action that he brought successfully against the South African government. He was at that time too old to undertake the journey, and I represented him for two days of cross-examination in Johannesburg.

He won huge damages in the case, but the summing-up was fair. Briefly, that his method was sound but his presentation of it misleading. Fortunately, the judges saw past his mode of presentation to the value of what he was actually doing.

Alexander retained to the end his immense teaching skill and patience. In the years before his death, his hard life took its toll, and he began to despair of his ideas ever being accepted without being watered down. The widespread application and importance of his Principle were not immediately obvious in the first half of this century. He had found it at first in his study of the *act of speaking,* and he made the fairly trite observation that the way people use their muscles affects the way their voices function. Trite because many schools of speech training, speech therapy, and drama devote themselves to just such a study of the mechanics of voice function. What was not trite about his observation was his analysis of the physical and psychological factors involved in USE, and his realization that by his method of detailed analysis a large number of psychological and physical disorders—disorders unconnected with the voice—would appear in a completely new light.

The Alexander Principle says that

USE AFFECTS FUNCTIONING.

USE

USE is the theme of this book.

You are sitting somewhere, perhaps lying somewhere, reading this book. Are you aware of how your hand is holding the book? If you direct your attention to your hand, you will become aware of the pressure of your fingers taking the weight of the book. How are you sitting? Are your knees crossed? Is the weight of your body more on one buttock than the other? Where are your elbows? As you run your eyes over the page, does your head move to alter your eye position or do just your eyes move? Where are your shoulder blades? How much muscle tension are you creating in your chest and forearms and generally throughout your body?

USE means the way we use our bodies as we live from moment to moment. Not only when we are moving, but when we are keeping still. Not only when we are speaking, but when we are thinking. Not only when we are making love, but when we are feeling or refusing to feel pleasure. Not only when we are communicating by gestures and attitudes, but when, unknown to ourselves, our bodily mood and disposition tell people what we are like and keep us that way whether we like it or not.

FUNCTIONING

FUNCTIONING is also the theme of this book. All of us are functioning—adequately, inadequately, happily, unhappily, healthily, unhealthily. A few case histories will give an idea of the sort of wrong functioning that accompanies wrong use.

By the time we reach adult life, if not before, most of us will have developed tension habits that are harmful. The habits at first may show themselves only as trifling inconsistencies of behavior, or perhaps as occasional muscular pain or clumsiness. Frequently, however, they appear as infuriating blockages that prevent us from giving our best just when we most need to, whether it be in the everyday business of personal relations or in more exacting situations like competitive sport, public speaking, making music, or making love. Dr. James P., a chest physician, has been worried for some time by increasing depression and a constant pain in his neck. He assuages them with liberal doses of alcohol and by the thanks of his grateful patients. He is a scholarly man who knows all about depression and psychosomatic pains in the neck. His own neck still hurts, and it is getting him down.

About twenty years ago, when he was a timid medical student, he opted for a rather pompous manner that involved straightening his neck, pulling his chin down onto his throat, and occasionally belching, preceded by a slight swallowing of air to provide the necessary ammunition. A few years later, he refined the head posture to include a deprecatory twist of his head to one side and a puffing out of his chest in front. A few years after that, he was making these movements even when he was alone and sitting quite still: the belching had become a habit, and, in between belching, he tightened his throat and restricted his breathing.

Dr. P. has already consulted his psychiatric colleagues and has reluctantly cut down on much of his work, since he finds it impossible to concentrate. There isn't the slightest possibility of getting rid of his neck pain until his strange muscular usages have been sorted out. Some of his problems are dealt with in Chapter 5.

The Student

Jane B., a nineteen-year-old, had been studying English literature at her university. At high school she had basically been a "good" girl, and was one of the two girls in her class who had never smoked or lost her virginity. After two days at the university, she turned up at home saying she couldn't stand it, but then reluctantly agreed to go back. (Her parents later wished that they had abided by their daughter's instinctive rejection.)

She found herself painfully unable to talk with other

people and she withdrew more and more into herself. At this point, like many other students, she could have chosen to fall in with the general permissive scene, and like many others, if her temperament had been unsuited to it, she might have sickened of it and made stable enjoyable relationships that used the social antidepressant drugs as an occasional pleasure rather than a constant haven.

Instead Jane B. cracked up. She wept almost continuously, not just with tears from her eyes but with an agonized contraction through her whole body. Her stomach contracted, her hands twisted and tensed, her eyes and head dropped down on her chest, and her shoulders lifted up toward her ears. The psychiatrists said it was "reactive depression" and treated her with shock therapy and antidepressant drugs. It was not until her USE was considered that the breakthrough to improved functioning became possible. The relationship of USE to mental functioning is described in Chapter 5.

The Journalist

Mrs. Elizabeth D. used to be a household name in the better Sunday newspapers in England—wittily informed and human, plagued with the problems of her wittily informed and human readers. An Oxbridge degree had neither kept her in the Shades of Academe nor precipitated her into the world of giggling revolutionaries. At the age of thirty-five, with a famous husband and growing children, she suddenly began to wonder what it was all about. She came to me ostensibly for help with her hobby of flute-playing—her breathing and her fingering were totally unpredictable—but a whole range of psychosomatic symptoms were soon being presented to me for appraisal. Full description might make her too identifiable, but her main trouble—the universal trouble —was her sex life. It has been said that at any given time you are in trouble because you are worrying about your sex life; or you are in real trouble because you are not worrying about your sex life.

Elizabeth's problem was fairly clear. She felt constantly very sexy, and could be triggered off into sexual excitement by quite small things, but when she began to engage in actual love activities, she would immediately go cold and dead. The harder she worked toward orgasm, the more irritated and less responsive she became.

The sexual problems in which muscular usage plays a prime part are dealt with in Chapter 6 (The Psycho-Mechanics of Sex), but it should not be thought that these are simply the problems of the tense pelvis—Wilhelm Reich's "frozen pelvis." Each of us has elaborated our own minutely variegated system of muscular usages not only in our pelvises but throughout the whole of our bodies—usages that are suddenly thrown up to demand their share of the picture at the most inconvenient moment, and to interfere with the balanced functioning we expect from our bodies.

The Schoolboy

Edward P. is eleven years old. Two years ago he felt a curious "thumping" at the back of his head, and when his mother became worried by what he told her, he got very upset himself. The school doctor could not explain it, nor could a whole battery of neurologists, orthopedic surgeons, and ear, nose, and throat specialists who were consulted. The young boy was by now becoming extremely hypochondriacal about it and would argue at length with his mother about how he had said the symptoms felt at such and such a time. Their doctor became heartily sick of it all, and a new doctor had little extra to offer. A close friend had heard of an osteopath who could do wonders, so the boy went to the osteopath to have his neck cricked week after week, and the "thumping" was quite a convenient reason not to undertake school activities when there was stress around. As is so in these cases, however—and as may have been so all along—Edward's pattern of muscular use deteriorated in an alarming way.

When he came to see me with his young mother, he could not keep his neck and shoulders still for more than a few seconds, and I was fascinated to see that his mother participated fully in this pattern of muscular twisting and wriggling. They communicated with each other by fractional shifts of muscular adjustment, in which one of them would counter the hints or suggestions of the other by a movement which in its turn had to be countered. This game of muscular Ping-Pong between the two was quite unconscious; it reminded me of a Jungian psychotherapist who had a habit of establishing rapport with her patients by a series of knowing wriggles and head nods that seemed to her like an exhibition of friendliness, but that must have felt like an irritating intrusion to the patient. The psychotherapist—whom I was treating for a muscle-tension state —said that when I taught her a balanced state of rest, she felt as if she weren't establishing proper rapport with her patients, although in fact they seemed to find it easier to talk to her.

Edward P. was not untypical of boys of his age. By the age of eleven, 70% of all boys and girls already show quite, marked muscular and posture deficiencies. Mostly these defects appear as passing inefficiencies and difficulties in learning; they become accentuated in emotional situations, and they presage an uneasy adolescence in which childhood faults become blown up into full-fledged defects. By the age of eighteen, only 5% of the population are free from defects, 15% have slight defects, 65% have quite severe defects, and 15% have very severe defects. These figures are based on my published surveys of boys and girls from secondary schools, and students from physical training, music, and drama colleges, some of whom might reasonably be expected to have a higher physical standard than the rest of the population. It is almost certain that you, the reader of this book, have quite pronounced defects of which you yourself are unconscious, and which your doctors, teachers, or parents did not notice, or did not worry about, or just accepted as an inevitable part of the way you are made.

These case histories all say the same thing: USE affects FUNCTIONING. The physician with his neck pain, the student with her depression, the journalist with her muscular frigidity, the schoolboy with his habit-spasm—all had been pathetically mishandled by their doctors. Diagnosis in their cases had been inadequate, not only because of a mistaken idea of what diagnosis should involve but because of a failure to observe and understand what is meant by USE.

William Harvey, in 1616, described the circulation of the blood, and thereby revolutionized medical thought. This did not mean that prior to that time the blood had not circulated and that it suddenly started circulating there and then. It had circulated for eons before Harvey first described— albeit imperfectly—what was going on. In the same way, the type of USE that Alexander described has been present for eons. Before Alexander much was known about it, but not in a way that could helpfully be applied to man's health.

It is a long way from William Harvey to Christiaan Barnard. What is written here will no doubt seem elementary in a hundred years' time, and indeed, since Alexander's death his procedures have been constantly refined; no doubt many more false leads will be attempted and have to be abandoned. It has to be stated clearly that the type of USE I describe in this book cannot be considered as the only right way. The USE I describe is the best I have been able to discover, and as I describe it, it works. But I assume —and hope—that far better ways will be found eventually of depicting and refining this new approach.

CHAPTER 2
Use and Mis-use

USE

Most of us are fatalistic about our bodies. We expect to grow up tall, short, plump, thin, weak, muscular, graceful, or clumsy. We expect when we are young that we will grow up and grow old, and that as we grow old our bodies will deteriorate. We think that our structural faults lie in our stars and in our parents, not in ourselves; that our body potential is immutably limited by our initial genetic program.

To some extent we are right, but to say this is not to have said much more than that the game of chess is boringly limited by the black and white squares.

The Alexander Principle insists that our will is potentially free. What is done with our genetic inheritance determines our future structure and performance. We use and mis-use our bodies in such simple matters as standing, sitting, and lying down, and even at this crude level there is USE that is beneficial and USE that is harmful. The basic structure of the personality, at its most minute and intimate level, is fashioned from our BODY USE.

ALEXANDER'S DISCOVERY OF WRONG USE

The Primary Control

Alexander's observation of his unconscious mis-use of the neck and head led him to term his improved USE the "primary control." He wrote in the *Lancet:* "When I was experimenting with various ways of using myself in an attempt to improve the functioning of my vocal organs, I discovered that a certain use of the head in relation to the neck and of the neck in relation to the torso . . . constituted a 'Primary Control' of the mechanisms as a whole."

Alexander and some of his supporters at one time seemed to impute an almost magical significance to the "primary control." Some of his medical friends gave him information about "controlling centers" in the midbrain in terms that seemed to imply a subjective awareness of such a center, which could exert a "primary control" over the rest of the body. Shades of Descartes and his "pineal body"!

Few people would find it helpful nowadays to talk about a "primary control," although in the past the phrase did emphasize the prime importance of a proper USE of the head and neck, at a time when anatomists and physiologists had no very clear account to give of the factors underlying balance. Fortunately the "primary control" hypothesis did not hold up the development of Alexander's practical teaching methods, although it certainly affected the way he taught.

Head Retraction

Alexander wrote further of his observations as follows:

> If you ask someone to sit down, you will observe, if you watch their actions closely, that there is an alteration in the position of the head, which is thrown back, whilst the neck is stiffened and shortened.

I thought I would see if this was in fact true. I had the opportunity to carry out an experiment with 108 young men,

1. Head pulling back into shoulders, as in figure 1.

aged between seventeen and twenty-two. (Plate 1 shows a young man sitting down. It can be seen that he is throwing his head backward in the process.) When I tested them, I fixed a tape measure to the back of their heads and made an ink mark over the prominent vertebra where the neck joins the chest at the back (Fig. 1a). I then asked them to sit down, and while they were sitting down I observed how much the tape measure moved down over the ink mark (Fig. 1b).

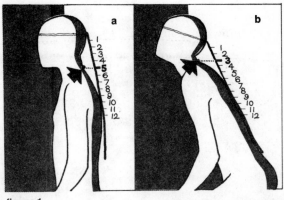

figure 1

Out of the 108, only one did not move the tape downward, 56 moved it down two inches or more, 43 between one and two inches, and 9 under an inch. The younger ones drew their heads back and down less than the older ones. What was even more interesting was that when I asked them to prevent this, only 11 of them were able to stop contracting their heads into their shoulders, however hard they tried.

Sir Charles Sherrington, the neurophysiologist, pointed out what a complicated thing it is to do even such a simple thing as sitting down:

To execute it must require the right degree of action of a great many muscles and nerves, some hundreds to thousands of nerve fibres, and perhaps a hundred times as many muscle fibres. Various parts of my brain are involved in the co-ordinative management of this, and in so doing, my brain's rightness of action rests on receiving and dispatching thousands of nerve messages, and on registering and adjusting pressures and tensions from various parts of me.[1]

It is not surprising that most of these young men could not change their habitual head movement simply by trying. We cannot alter our habitual way of doing things simply by deciding to do them some other way. Our will is potentially free, but to free it for effective action we need certain principles of USE on which to base our actions.

THE USE OF THE HEAD

One hundred and seven of the 108 young men showed this particular use of the head in which the skull was pulled back on the neck. The first thing to decide is whether or not such a habitual use of the head and neck is important. Consider this: the whole region at the base of the neck, both back and front, is a veritable maelstrom of muscular coordination. It is here that those most inadequate evolutionary adaptations—the shoulders and upper arms—will exert their distorting influence during the many activities in which we engage. Here faulty patterns in breathing can throw the muscles of the lower neck and upper ribs into excessive spasm. It is here that mechanisms of speech and swallowing require a reasonably good vertebral posture if the esophagus and trachea and associated vocal structures are to function well. Close to this region blood vessels and nerves of great importance and complexity pass: blood vessels to the base of the brain, nerve ganglia which affect breathing and heart rate and blood pressure, nerve roots which with increasing age become more and more liable to compression. It is here that a large percentage of the readers of this book will have arthritis by the time they are 55 (and many of them much younger than that), and it is from here that the head itself—the structure which carries man's most important sensory equipment of sight and hearing, taste and smell, and balance—has to be coordinated at rest and in movement.

Here mis-use most frequently starts. And here we must start if we are to correct the multitudinous mis-uses which the rest of the body can throw up. In terms of the Alexander Principle, it is only when this primary mis-use is dealt with that we shall see what the answers to an expanding range of questions are.

In the past, the hump has been thought of as a dull, inert, fleshy region, with little of interest to offer except to the painter or shot-putter or dowager pearl-wearer. When improved use has been established, the hump region simply provides a context within which other functioning can take place.

What produces the hump? Excessive and wrongly distributed muscle tension. By habitually moving and keeping still in certain ways, we gradually alter our physique. Our manner of USE at rest and during movement contains a substantial record of all the basic habits we have laid down over the years. In most people, the hump is a tangible witness to a lifetime of mis-use.

The phenomenon of head retraction which Alexander first noticed is a symptom of pre-existent muscle tension, not the cause of it. Alexander, with simple clarity, proposed that if only people could stop pulling their heads back whenever they reacted, all would be well, and he concentrated his efforts on training both himself and his pupils to stop doing just that.

Let us glance at the collection of sideways X-rays of the head and neck (Plate 2). In none of these X-rays did the radiologist mention the USE, since few radiologists are trained to comment on it. From medical reports and records, it might be assumed that the USE of these necks was to all intents the same, since (apart, perhaps, from mention of disk-narrowing) no comment was made on the relationship of head to neck or of the component vertebrae to each other. Yet they are very different necks indeed.

Plates 2a and 2b show a neck which is dropped markedly forward, and the skull pulled back. (Fig. 2c shows this diagrammatically.)

2. (a.) Neck collapsed forward.   (b.) Head back, upper neck forward, lower neck back.

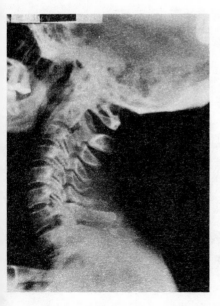 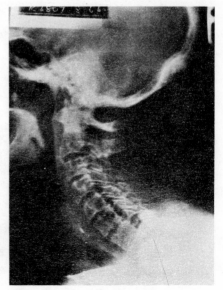

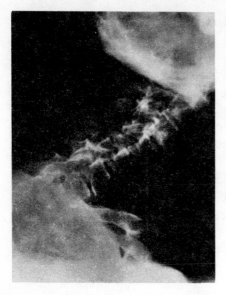

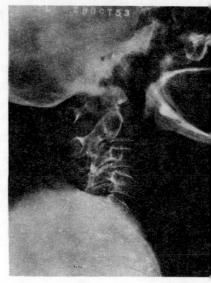

(c.) Head pulled back.

(d.) Lower neck collapsed out of sight.

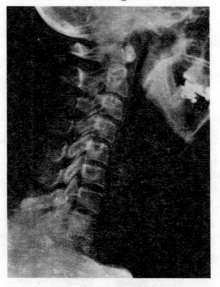

(e.) Overstraightened neck.
Fourth vertebra slipped forward on fifth.

In X-ray Plate 2c the neck is dropped even further.

In X-ray Plate 2d note that the collapse forward is so great that only five vertebrae are showing.

In X-ray Plate 2e the neck is overstraightened.

Let us look at a head and neck from the back and add a few more vertebrae—those in the hump at the upper part of the chest, the "dorsal spine," as it is called (Fig. 2e).

Look at your head and neck in a mirror. Many people develop a habit of pulling one ear slightly down toward the shoulder (Fig. 2f). Notice the level of the lobe of the ear. If you do pull one ear down, you will develop a compensatory twist in the neck, usually at the lower part of the neck and upper part of the dorsal spine. It happens to be a fact that this is a difficult place to X-ray, at least in routine X-rays of the neck and chest. Either the neck is X-rayed or the chest is X-rayed—the junction area tends to be ignored. Quite small twists in this area (a cervico-dorsal scoliosis) tend to be ignored, but they indicate considerable upsets in the muscle balance in the neck (Plate 3).

3. Sideways twist at base of neck (*see* Plate 5).

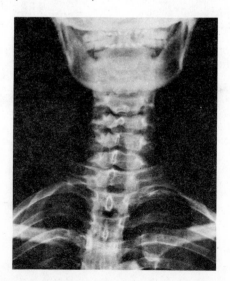

The Head and Neck

Let us take a schematic head and look at it sideways (fig. 2a). Let us take the seven neck vertebrae which connect it to the chest (fig. 2b). Now let us look again at the collection of sideways X-rays of the head and neck (Plate 2). The most common mis-use involves a pull of the head back and a drop forward of the neck (Plate 2a, b, c, d, and fig. 2c) but there are many variations. Sometimes there is an overstraightening of the neck (Plate 2e, f, and fig. 2d).

Let us look at a head and neck from the *back* and add a few more verte-brae—those in the "hump" at the upper part of the chest at the back (fig. 2e).

Many people will be able to see in a mirror that they have developed a habit of slightly pulling one ear down toward the shoulder (fig. 2f), as shown by the level of the earlobe. If this occurs it leads to a compensatory twist in the neck, usually in the lower part of the neck and the "hump."

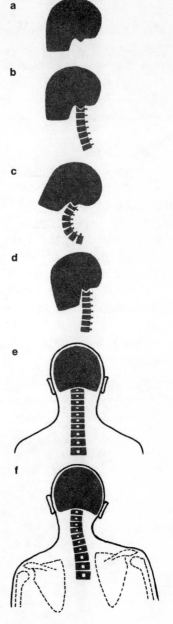

figure 2

Look at the line of muscles as they come out of your neck toward the shoulder (Fig. 3a).

The line will probably be lower on one side than the other, not just because being right- or left-handed has made the muscle bigger, but because of the structural mis-use— the scoliosis.

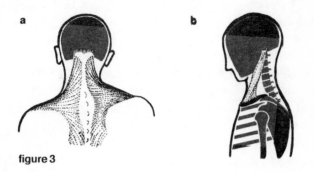

figure 3

With this imbalance, there will probably be more tension on one side of the neck in the back than on the other side (a fruitful source of headache and neck tension pain), or there will be more tension in one sterno-mastoid muscle, in front, than on the other side. The sterno-mastoid is the thin muscle that runs from your mastoid bone to the top of the breastbone. If you pull your chin down onto your throat (Fig. 3b) and touch your fingers just above the inner ends of the collarbones, you will feel it contract. Needless to say, many other muscles on the sides of the neck and below the chin will contract if you pull your chin down in this manner.

Usually, if the head pulls to one side, it will also rotate slightly, so that someone looking at you from the back would see more of your jaw on one side than the other. An established rotation or sideways contraction of the head will lead to an asymmetry in your face and perhaps to slight occlusion troubles, since your jaw will be opening sideways. And to that most distressing symptom, the clicking jaw.

While we are discussing the head, look at your eyes. Are you frowning? There may be wrinkles, because of age, but a deeply fixed frown can usually be released a little without loss of social seriousness (if, indeed, this type of frowning seriousness is ever needed). And the jaws may be held too tightly together—leading in some cases to tooth-grinding. If the lower jaw is dropped, there will be less tension. When the jaw is closed, the lower teeth should not touch the upper teeth, but should lie just behind them. When the jaw opens, it should first drop a very small distance and then move slightly forward, as a bulldog holds his lower teeth pushed forward. Many jaws are permanently held in an "undershot" position, many are held back into the throat, not because the trait is inherited but because of habit. And, of course, some people feel their chins are big and ugly and hold them in to try to make them look smaller—a dubious cosmetic advantage for which high cost is paid in terms of tension and fixation.

While we are on the topic of jaws, we must say a word about stammering. In recent years, leading speech therapists have realized and acknowledged how fundamental the Alexander Principle is in their re-educational work, and I have seen many intractable stammers greatly helped by re-education along these lines. Most of the leading speech-training colleges in Britain now know about and use the Principle as a fundamental part of their training.

Mis-use elsewhere can only be adequately dealt with after the correction of mis-use of the head and neck. To para-phrase Gilbert Ryle: "When, in the case of a range of problems of bodily mis-use, it is clear that none of them can be dealt with or perhaps even clearly formulated before some anterior problem is dealt with, then the need to solve this anterior problem can be termed a principle."

It is apparent from this that we have to start by asking the right questions about our body. So let us, as systematically as possible, consider some of the most common and obvious mis-uses that can be detected by almost anyone who looks for them.

THE CHEST

It is easy to develop a sideways twist where the neck joins the back (Fig. 4). This is usually accompanied by a throwing of the chest sideways in the opposite direction

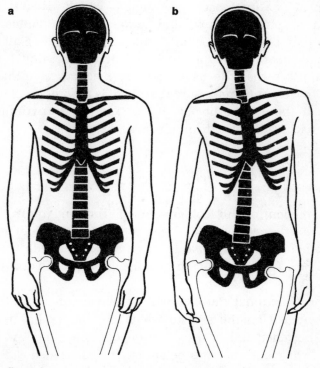

figure 4

to the head. The chest (and collarbones in front), which should lie something like Fig. 4a, instead lies something like Fig. 4b.

The collarbone on the side to which it is pushed over may be slightly higher than the other (although *both* collarbones may already be too high because of shoulder tension). The angle between your ribs will be sharper on one side than the other, and in fact the chest may not be so inflated on that side as on the other, and the cartilage that joins the front of the lower ribs may be felt pushing forward more than on the other side. Such chest twists and rotations are frequently unobserved by doctors, and many patients suffer from distressing pain in the chest—sometimes labeled "pleurodynia" or "intercostal neuralgia"—which does not respond to physiotherapy, and leaves lurking doubts that there may be a heart or lung pathology in spite of all tests showing heart and lungs to be clear. (Everything I write presupposes that the usual obvious medical examinations are carried out to make sure that there is no gross pathology. Even if there is pathology, it can rarely do anything but good to consider also the manner of USE.)

THE ABDOMEN

If you continue to look at yourself front on, you may perhaps notice that one side of your abdomen is straighter than the other—that you have less "waist" on one side than on the other. This follows from the displacement of your thorax sideways.

The abdominal muscles will be overstretched and overstraightened on the side to which the thorax has moved, and shortened and "waisted" on the opposite side. And often when this happens, the pelvis on the shortened side will be contracted up toward the chest.

Osteopaths often attribute such twists to a short leg, and usually this is because in an X-ray the pelvis is found to be tilted up more on one side than on the other. There are indeed *some* shortened legs, markedly so in cases after fractures or polio or arthritis, etc. Usually, though, an inaccurate measurement of the *true* length of the leg will have been made (i.e., it was measured from the wrong bony points), and the remedy of building up the shoe to lengthen the supposedly short leg will do little to correct an imbalance that stems from a sideways displacement of the neck and chest.

4. Slump and curvature of the spine.

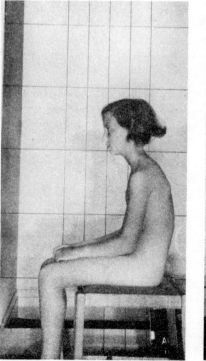 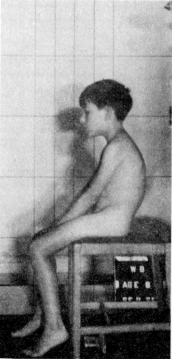

An overcontraction of muscles may also be found in the front of the abdomen. In addition to acting as a form of "muscular armor," which, by continued use, attempts to counteract feelings of butterflies or anxiety or sexual stirrings, the overcontraction will occasionally give rise to abdominal pain. The diagnosis of "spastic colon" is very often accompanied by such unnoticed abdominal mis-use, and many people with this distressing condition can be helped, and may avoid needless and fruitless abdominal surgery.

Abdominal laxity and general flabbiness are more often the rule in the middle-aged, and to understand this we need to look once more at our spines and our stance side on.

Plate 4 shows two typically slumping children. This is the rule, not the exception, in most schools. Alertness at first is made possible by the natural ongoing vitality of most of us; but for many schoolchildren, the hours in class are hours of unmitigated boredom, punctuated by bouts of fear and aggression. Added to which the accent on learning to read and write involves provision of a desk, toward which the eyes and head will tend to drop.* In fact, there will be a position of hump where the neck joins the chest, plus the slumping of the lower back and collapse of the rib cage (Fig. 5a).

The slumped head posture becomes habitual, so that when the eyes are raised to look ahead it has to be accomplished by an increase in the forward curve in the neck (Fig. 5b).

But the habit of holding the eyes down may persist until eventually the back of the skull begins to be *held* contracted back into the upper neck in order to look straight ahead (Fig. 5c).

* A nice verbatim account by Crispin, aged nine: "Nearly all the children at school sit with their spines all curled up. That can't be good, can it? Sometimes the teacher tells us to sit up straight and when we ask her why her back is all curved she says she is relaxing."

In other words, the plane of the eyes is altered more by moving the level of the head than by moving the eyes (although they will move a little).

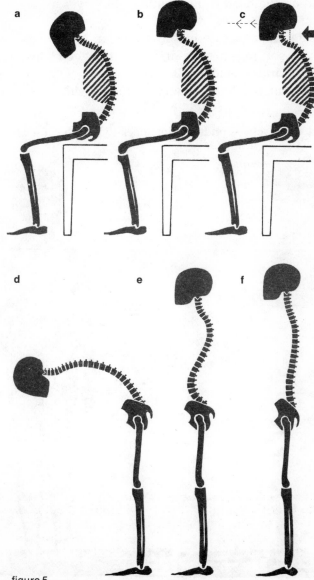

figure 5

What happens when the child stands up?

When he stands up, he cannot simply keep a continuous rounded curve down the back (Fig. 5d). And he makes a necessary (but wrong) compensation in the lower back. If we add on the head compensation, this gives us Fig. 5e, instead of the good USE in Fig. 5f.

The familiar picture of the arched-in lower back, which is so common in schoolchildren over the age of five, is seen in Plates 5 and 6 in older children.

And from the back view we see the sideways scoliotic

5. Lordosis in schoolchildren. Note neck twist in boy (*see* Plate 3).

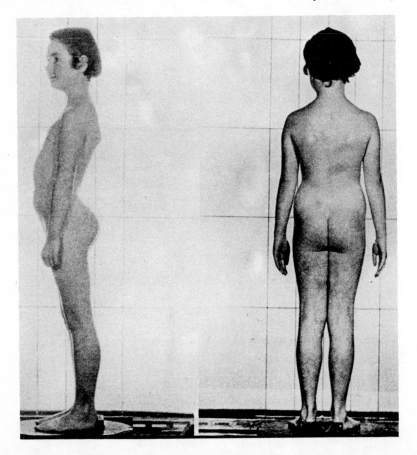

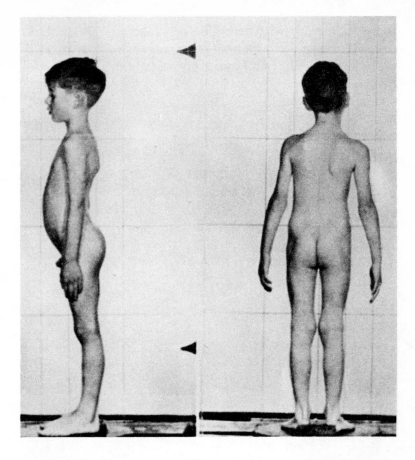

twists that start in the neck (Plate 5) and are compensated wrongly in the chest and lower back.

This combination of lordosis (arched-in back) plus scoliosis (sideways curvature) will persist into adult life (Plates 7 and 12) and will usually be present when there is chronic back pain. (For the most part, it is only in the *acutely* painful back that the lumbar curve is flattened by spasm—a fact that has led some orthopedic surgeons to encourage back-arching in an effort to overcome such flattening.) The pathetic picture in Plate 8 shows a patient (who has already undergone a back operation) being encouraged to do just the things that will make his already dreadful posture much worse.

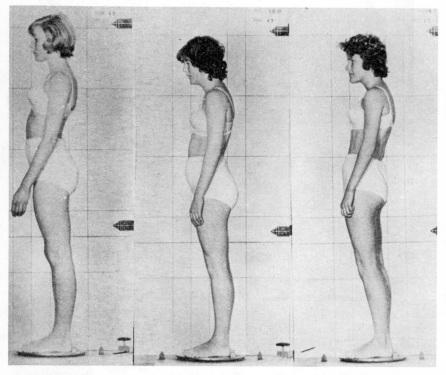

6. Three schoolgirls considered by their teachers to have good posture. Note humps.

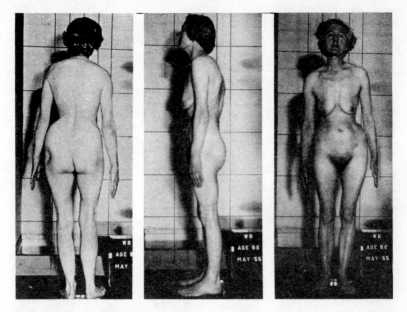

7. Elderly woman. Chest displaced to right, pelvis to left. Note neck collapse and tense sterno-mastoid muscle.

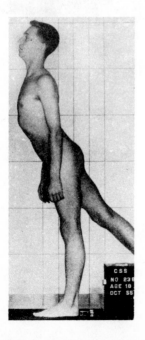

8. Patient with arched back doing wrong exercise.

PELVIS AND LEGS

The pelvis is a most difficult bone to visualize to oneself, as Fig. 6 will indicate.

By far the commonest general mis-use of the pelvis involves pulling the buttocks backward and upward toward the lower back—part of the process of arching the back inward that we have already noticed. In addition, just like the skull, the pelvis may be tilted up more on one side and it may be rotated back on one side.

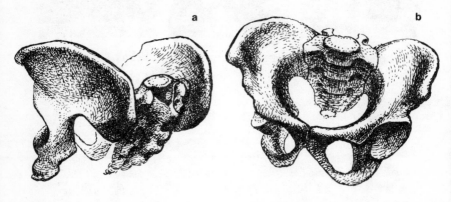

figure 6

The pelvic muscles are extremely complex (Fig. 7): on the inside they include the muscles that connect up the lower back with the perineum and legs (Figs. 7a and 7b), and on the outside the small and big muscles that are responsible for standing, walking, running, and jumping. One should perhaps make the point here that when you are sitting, your knees should never be crossed. If they are crossed, it will involve a mis-use of the muscles that connect the lower back to the upper part of the thigh (Figs. 7c and 7d). Crossing the ankles is far less likely to involve mis-use.

If you stand with your back to a wall (Fig. 8), with your heels about two inches in front of it, and feet about eighteen

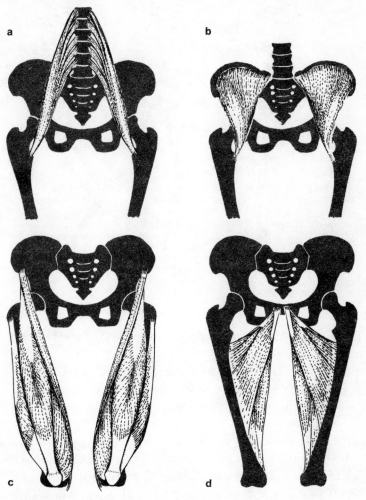

a

b

c

d

figure 7

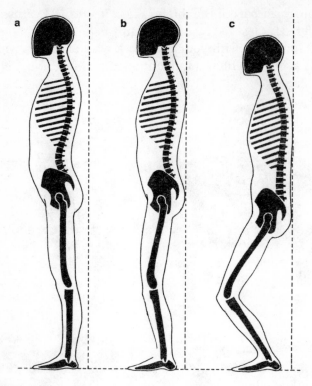

figure 8

inches apart, you can begin to notice and identify some of your defects.

Sway your body back to the wall, keeping your toes on the ground. Your shoulder blades *and* your buttocks should hit the wall simultaneously. If you are rotated, one side will hit the wall first; if your pelvis is usually carried too far forward, your shoulders will hit the wall but not your buttocks.

If the buttocks are not touching the wall, bring them back to the wall. You may notice now that there is a big gap between your lower back and the wall. This gap will disappear if you bend both your knees forward (keeping your heels on the ground) and, at the same time, drop your buttocks and tip the sexual organs more toward the front, rather than toward the floor. If you find this position tiring after a short time, then you are indeed in a mis-used state! But you will be gratified to notice that your flabby dropped-forward stomach has taken on a slimmer appearance. You may also find that the back of your skull is touching the wall. This is a mis-use—Alexander's basic fault of "head retraction," as described earlier in this chapter.

Notice, in this position, whether the arches of your feet are flattened. You can probably unflatten them if, with the knees still bent, you turn your kneecaps outward, rather as the eyeballs can be squinted out at the sides. This will also tend to correct bowleg (tibial torsion).

Now slowly straighten your knees, but do not brace them back when you are standing fully erect. *The knees should never be braced back when standing*, but should always be slightly bent; the same applies to walking.

At this point, there should be only a slight arch in the lower back, depending on your particular build and avoirdupois. You can now take your body away from the wall, keeping your feet where they were. In taking the body thus forward, the head should lead the movement, not the chest or abdomen.

If you now bring the feet together, you are in a position to detect faults in your walking pattern. Place two high-backed chairs in front of you (Fig. 9) and hold them with the tips of the fingers and thumb, and with the elbows well out. Begin to walk with the right leg by raising the right knee a little, so that the right heel leaves the ground. But as you do this there will be a slight transfer of weight to the left leg to enable the right foot to leave the ground. Many people will find that instead of getting the right foot off the ground by bending the right knee, they pull the right side of the pelvis up toward the right side of the chest (Fig. 9b).

You will detect this happening by the excessive pressure that is made through one of the hands holding the chair. There should be no disturbance of the upper body and arms

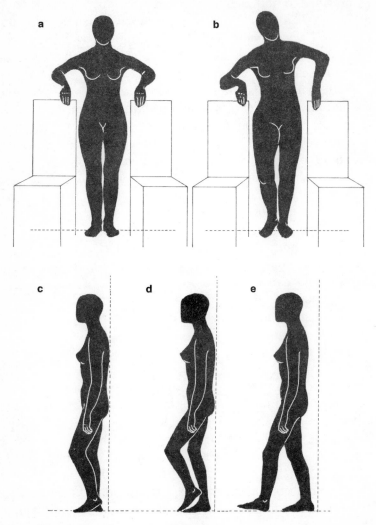

figure 9

when this initial movement of bending the knee is made (Fig. 9c).

The next stage of walking is simply to go on bending the knee until only the tip of the big toe is left touching the ground (Fig. 9d); then, as the whole body moves forward, the foot leaves the ground and should be placed in front with the *heel* touching the ground just before the sole of the foot touches (Fig. 9e). The knee should not be braced back, as in a "goosestep"; and if the sole hits the ground first, it will usually have involved too much arching of the lower back. With the heel-toe action, it is possible to maintain a use of the lower back in which it is directed "up and back"—a point that will be elaborated in the next chapter.

Such a maneuver is intended not to teach you how to walk, but simply to indicate at this stage how to detect faults in your walking pattern. A fully integrated pattern of walking would involve very close attention to the upper part of the body, not just to the legs. It is, of course, easier if you have the help of a teacher who can show you how to hold the top of each chair between your fingers and hands so that you do not create undue tension in the head, neck, shoulders, and arms.

SHOULDERS AND ARMS

There is no particular reason except convenience for leaving a consideration of shoulders and arms to this point. Indeed, they are, for most people, an important site of misuse, since they are involved in so much of the life of civilized man. Fig. 10 shows the muscles which often distort the USE of the shoulder blades.

In most people, the shoulder blades are drawn up toward the back of the neck during movement and, eventually, even at rest. They will often also be pulled together too much, either because of wrong instruction at school—to "pull your shoulders together"—or else because in the sedentary unenergetic life most people lead the chest cage is relatively unexpanded, and the shoulder blades, which should lie flat and widened across the back of the properly expanded chest, tend to come together and become winged when the chest is unexpanded. (You will perhaps feel the bottom end of a shoulder blade sticking out if you put one hand behind your back and stretch it across to touch the opposite shoulder blade.)

The winged position of the shoulder blades can be temporarily counteracted by raising the hands and arms forward. This movement (which takes place when you are holding the top of a chair, as previously described) will usually cause the shoulder blades to lie flat on the back of the chest—a position in which they should lie even when the arms hang to the side. When you are holding a chair in this manner, the elbows should be turned well away from the body, the cubital fossa (the bend of the elbows) facing the side of the body. The position may feel round-shouldered, but that is because the "hump" is now more obvious and no longer disguised by a spurious squaring of the shoulders. The round-shouldered appearance is to be corrected by lengthening off the hump, not by pulling the shoulders together.

Pulling the shoulder blades together is usually accompanied by holding them up too tightly at the back of the neck and hump, and since the upper part of the chest is conical and narrower than the lower chest, the shoulder blades will be pulled inward toward the hump as they rise up over the chest. Obviously, the tension has to be released by a slight dropping and widening of the shoulder blades. Most people find it difficult to do this without slumping their lower back at the same time. So not only do the shoulders have to be released and widened, but the back has, at the

a   b

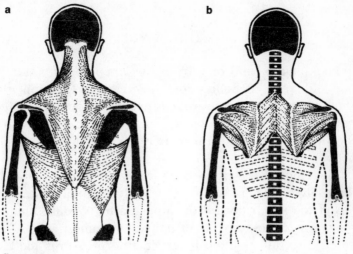

figure 10

same time, to lengthen (without arching) and to widen out
to support the shoulders, a process that is facilitated if the
chest cage is expanded to widen across the back.

A great deal of emotional tension is expressed in the
shoulders. Dorothy Tutin told me that she played Joan of
Arc with the shoulders slightly raised and fixed to give a
feeling of defiance. A whole range of most subtle emotions
are manifested in the shoulders—shrugs, aggressive threat-
enings, or resignation and nostalgia—from, say, a slight
release of the upper chest muscles as they insert into the
upper arm in the armpit.

THE ARMS

Look at the bend of your elbow when you are standing. It should not be facing forward at rest. The upper arm should turn slightly inward, so that the elbow turns slightly out and away from the body. If the shoulders are slumped, the upper arms will also usually be held too close to the body.

The front of the elbow is a place where most people hold themselves far too fixed, so that the forearm, at rest, may be flexed too much toward the upper arm. We use our arms for many of our activities of daily living, and they gradually adopt a resting position in which the forearm is too tense, the elbow a little too bent, and the hand not sufficiently straightened out. A line from the inside of the elbow which can be drawn down, via the inner border of the wrist, to the end of the thumb, should be almost straight, so that the fingers, at rest, can be straightened and turned slightly away from the thumb. Driving a car, playing a musical instrument, handling tools and objects of all kinds can be most economically carried out from this resting position, which will also involve a broadening of the palm of the hand and a separating of the fingers. One should endeavor to adjust the height and position of desks, musical instruments, display panels on workbenches, etc., so that good use of the arm and hand is not hampered. And in writing and typewriting, there should not be too much deviation from the good use of the shoulders, arms, and hands. In treating medical conditions like the stiff "frozen" shoulder, tennis elbow, and tenosynovitis of the wrist, it is of paramount importance to establish correct habits of using the whole upper limb, and to insure adequate postural support for it from the trunk. Likewise in games and athletic activities, it is essential to learn a basic resting use of the arms and shoulders. A consideration of mis-uses may give a clue to persistent putting errors or slicing of the golf ball, or patches of erratic serving and smashing in tennis.

THE SEDENTARY LIFE

Few of us will spend more than an hour or so at a time without sitting down. For many people, more of their working day is spent sitting down than moving—except, of course, for young children who, once they can walk, can only be made to sit still for a short time if they are restrained in highchairs and seat harnesses, or by their mothers' hands and arms. The young child instinctively moves and explores and communicates as soon as it wakes, and it will continue to do this until it is tired, or until it has been rebuked or restricted into a stillness that is socially more convenient. Such restriction is an inevitable feature of school life, and eventually the growing child may well be sitting at a desk for hours on end, in a class with forty other children. Most of the children in the classroom will be sitting in a collapsed state, with the weight of the trunk supported through the elbows and shoulders. The sedentary life has begun.

If so much of our life is spent in a sedentary position— and most of the men and women in government, industry, medicine, law, music, education, and so on, will have spent many years sitting down while they equipped themselves for their job—it would seem important to consider how we use ourselves in that position.

SITTING DOWN

Over 99% of us, as exemplified by the 108 young men —and confirmed by studies on all age groups from puberty upward—pull the back of the skull down into the back of the neck as we sit down and stand up. Usually—unless as actors or dancers we have had to think carefully about it—we are relatively unaware of how we use our bodies as we are carrying out our daily activities. When we want to sit down, we walk to the available seat, rapidly gauge the seat height, and plant our bottoms without further ado in such a way as to avoid other people and other objects and without showing too much thigh. In the process, the head usually pulls back and the spine becomes curved. When the seat has been reached, there are a few shuffles and wiggles to eliminate the creeping and crinkling of clothing, and then the body is allowed to collapse while the head and neck are kept in a position that will allow social intercourse or reading or writing. This more often than not involves using the arms and shoulders as struts to support the col-lapsed body. For eating, the face drops down toward the plate. For watching television, once the initial hypnosis has been induced, the body is collapsed to the lowest point of slump at which the eyes can look ahead out of their sockets. The miracle is that human beings survive it at all. The tragedy is that they know no better, and by the time their bodies begin to cry out "Enough, enough," they are set in their ways and in their social commitments.

SLUMP

Sitting down has been mentioned first because so much of our time is spent using ourselves in this position, and also because the mis-use in this position is so obvious. When Alexander studied his head movements and positions during speech, the mis-use was not so obvious, although Plates 5a and 5b show only too clearly how gross the wrong movements of the head can be. And if we consider the picture of the dentist in Plate 9 and observe his head and neck position as he bends over a "patient," it is clear that his

9. Dentist's hump from bending over patients.

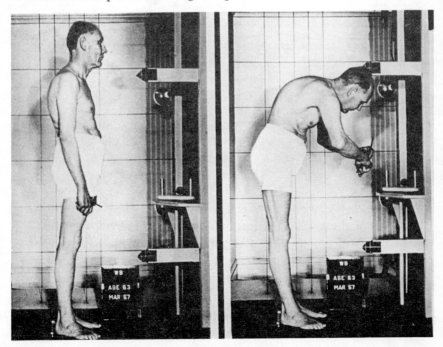

mis-use consists of dropping his neck forward, and collapsing his upper back into a curve. The movements can be
illustrated by the hand and wrist (Fig. 11). The dropping
forward of the wrist corresponds to the dropping forward
of the neck, and this is shown on a skull in Fig. 11b. Perhaps
the movements can be more clearly seen in X-rays of the

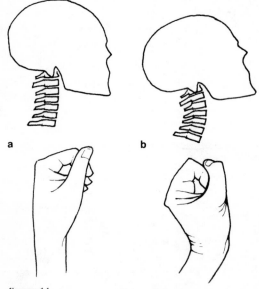

a   b

figure 11

neck (Plates 2a and 2b). The collapsed neck leads to a throwing in of the back—the lordosis which is so obvious in many
people and which remedial gymnasts try in vain to correct
in schoolchildren. The almost pandemic complaint of low
back pain (ranging from housewives' lumbago to the out-
right slipped disk) cannot be adequately treated by simply
concentrating on the lower back. In the majority of cases,
the lower back deformity is consequent on a deformity in

the hump. Only when the mis-use in the upper part of the body is corrected can there be the most efficient stabilizing of the lower back.

THE BEGINNINGS OF MIS-USE

From the moment of birth, the helpless child is dependent on the handling and the ideas of its mother. It is picked up jerkily or smoothly, crossly or kindly; its head and back are supported carefully or ignorantly. It lies face down or face up, according to fashion. It is allowed to yell or it is picked up on demand. It connects with the mother, on breast or bottle, and as it suckles, it likes to gaze long and deep into the mother's eyes, with a unified visual connection which it may never know again. But, in the main, its connection is kinesthetic, through muscles and movement, and it is quick to pick up feelings of tension, timidity, or rejection from the bodily rather than the visual contact, and especially from the mother's hands, since hands are a most powerful stimulus toward good or bad USE.

As the nervous system develops, the stage of sitting up is reached. One of Alexander's earliest teachers, Alma Frank, carried out a painstaking study of how children first sit up. It showed that if children are made to sit up before their nervous systems have adequately matured, they loll about, with the beginnings of mis-use, and their backs develop a sideways curvature. She took some beautiful pictures of children who were left to adopt the sitting-up position on their own, at their own chosen time. She showed that if they were left alone, they would adopt a balanced upright position of the back, with the head in the position of Alexander's "primary control."

The child should be left to initiate movements in its own time. To pull a child up by the arms too soon is to ask for mis-use. By the age of twelve months, over 90% of children develop a sideways curvature in their backs. The urge to place a child on a pot and leave it sitting there hopefully should be restrained until such time as it can support its back properly without lolling and collapsing. Similarly, the various achievements of standing and taking the first steps should not be hurried. The child should not be "stood up" or encouraged to walk until its *own* balanced USE enables it to do so.

THE STANDING CHILD

There are few more beautiful sights than the well-USED child standing with legs slightly flexed in the Alexander balance and with the vertebral column well back, counterbalanced by the head. By the age of two and a half or three years, things for most children are already beginning to go sadly wrong.

The child at this age will have adopted many of the tempos and tensions of the parents. The family mood—or the mood of one dominant parent—will be inducing its associated posture in the child. This process will continue with us for all of our lives, since if we are to share the constructions that people we admire put on things, we are eventually forced to share something of their manner of USE—a "posture-swapping," in which they may also adopt something of our posture. We imitate the attitudes of those we admire in order to make contact easier: it is through USE that we construe our surroundings, and since a major part of our connecting up with other people consists of an attempt to share the construction they put on things, we have to adapt our USE to theirs. In a situation in which we are dominant, they will adapt their USE to ours: "posture-swapping" is rarely fifty-fifty; it tends to favor the dominant person.

The outcome of this projective posture-swapping will be a personally idiosyncratic mixture of tensions and predispositions of structures and potential attitudes, an amalgam of nature and not so much nurture as selective preference on the part of the *child* as he brings up his parents as best he can!

Various physical education colleges and local education authorities in England have, over the years, allowed me to carry out studies on their students and schoolchildren. A few years ago, as a medical member of the National Committee for Movement Training, I attempted to assess the physiological and psychological effects of various types of physical education.

The *pro forma* on page 52 has proved useful as a rough guide to assessing a given person's defects, and it has been adopted by educational authorities in their remedial work. It can be scored on a simple basis of one, two, or three marks, according to the severity of the defect. Most of these posture studies have been carried out with the help of Professor Tanner, of the Institute of Child Health. His book *Growth and Adolescence* will give an indication of the detail in which such studies are made.

Surveys were conducted at some of the leading physical education colleges in England, where a high physical standard is required at entry and which draw on some of the best athletes and games players in the country. This group of students have applied themselves from an early age to the development of their bodies, and they are destined to become physical education teachers all over the country.

When photographic analyses of their faults were made, a definite pattern of well-defined categories appeared: those scoring 0–3, who have excellent USE; those scoring 4–5, who have some slight defects; those scoring 6–9, who show severe defects; those scoring 10–14, who show very severe defects; and those over 15, who show really gross deformity. In a group of 112 physical education students, the majority —62%—showed severe defects, 11.5% showed slight defects, and 26.5% showed very severe defects. There were no students in the top grade, none in the lowest grade. Similar figures were obtained from groups of male and female drama students.[2]

Region	Fault	Score	Fault	Score
HEAD	Poked		Tilted	
	Retracted		Pulled Down	
SHOULDERS	Raised		Rotation	
	Dropped		Pulled Together	
PELVIS	Tilt		Forward Carriage	
	Rotation		Gluteal Asymmetry	
SPINE	Scoliosis		Lateral Curvature or Thorax Displacement	
	Kyphosis		Lordosis	
STANCE	Hyperextended Knees		Forward Inclination	
	Internal Rotation Knees		Symmetry	
TENSION	Specific			
	General			

On the basis of such studies, it is clear that whatever methods are being used in our schools, the end results, even in the best students, are not good. The idea that healthy natural outdoor life with plenty of fresh air and exercise will insure a reasonably good USE is simply not true; we see how high the incidence of defects is in physical education students. Even if it were true, the main problem would still be how to establish a USE that would withstand the strain of living in a civilization in which the healthy life may not be easily available.

The figures of wrong USE in students are alarming, but equally alarming are the figures which were obtained by the National Committee for Movement Training of the USE of children in secondary schools. This study was made in schools of Hertfordshire and, in addition to a whole battery of physiological and psychological tests, I carried out a survey of postural and tension defects.[3] The committee's comments at the end of the study were encouraging: "The main hope for the future seems to be the kind of measurements and ratings that Dr. Barlow and his colleagues can make."

In a world survey of physical education methods that was conducted in the United Kingdom, the United States, Australia, and the Soviet Union, the covering report was concluded by an account of the work that Professor Tanner and I have carried out. The report quoted me as follows: "At present, Physical Education training does not leave its pupils with either the knowledge or the desire to maintain healthful activity in advancing years. The problem of adult deterioration under civilized conditions is far more important than the problem of providing healthful outlets for the young. Physical Education has failed unless the adult both desires and is able to maintain good USE throughout his life."

To learn the Alexander Principle unaided is difficult, and

accordingly it is vital that this knowledge should eventually be available at the school level. Just how it is to be fitted in will be a matter for individual schools. One is tempted to feel that the Principle is too strong a medicine for some schools at present. However, through the patience and skill of certain Alexander teachers, who have quietly worked to prove to other school staff just how valuable their contribution can be, it does seem now that the Principle can be acceptably incorporated into many schools and that the process will be mutually helpful.

In recent years, Alexander teachers have been added to the staff of four colleges—the Royal College of Music (where most of my early research was done), the Royal Academy of Dramatic Art, New College of Speech and Drama, and Guildhall. The Inner London Education Authority has recognized the Alexander Institute for provision of major county awards—a move that may do something to satisfy the huge increase in demand for trained teachers. A recent survey in America said "probably the oldest and best known of the self-use systems is that developed by Alexander. It is impossible to do any work in self-use today without including kinesiology" (*Drama Review*, March 1972, p. 18). But, in the main, most Alexander training is still carried out by individual teachers who work privately. In the past, it has often been that when a new educational need has arisen, it first had to be dealt with in the private sector, rather than by the state. Only when the evidence of its need has become incontrovertible have the institutions joined in.

The evidence is now quite incontrovertible. We are witnessing a widespread deterioration in USE that begins at an early age, and that present educational methods are doing little to prevent. Most people have lost good USE by the time they are past early childhood. Nobody notices it until the defects have become severe. Many family situations are bound to produce tensions in children, but the maintenance of good USE is difficult even for the lucky one whose parents provide a balanced environment. It is difficult for children to "keep their heads" when they are surrounded by people who are monstrous monuments of mis-use.

CHAPTER 3

Balance and Rest

BALANCE

Among the bosoms and bottoms of seaside picture postcards there used to be one of a decrepit old man standing unsteadily in a doctor's surgery, legs splayed, holding on to the furniture, and saying, "Well, Doctor, how do I stand?" and receiving the inevitable answer, "Honestly, I can't imagine." When I look at the hunched backs, twisted spines, and fixed pelvises, and the hopelessly inadequate legs and feet which trudge through my clinic, I also often find it hard to imagine just how they manage to stand at all!

Balance for most people is not a question of tightrope perfection, or ski-jumping precision, or the pas de deux, or the coolness of the mountaineer. It is possible to sit, stand, walk, and indeed to perform highly skilled tasks and yet be wrongly balanced. The skater in Plate 10 can do something that most people would find impossible. She earns her living by bending double and then skating backward in order to pick up a handkerchief from the ice with her teeth. Obviously she has a keenly developed coordination for this and similar activities, yet her balanced USE of herself is wrong.

Close analysis of the photographs shows that her rib cage is twisted over to one side, not only when she bends but when she is standing still. Had it not been for the fact that

10. Skater unconsciously twisting her back when bending.

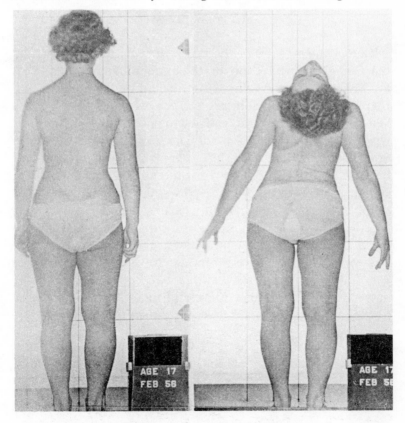

she eventually developed pain in her back while skating, she would have been totally unaware of this imbalance. Indeed her dance teacher, her doctor, and an orthopedic specialist had not noticed the twist, and she was unable to stop her pain until she learned how to use her back with a more symmetrical balance. Like most people, the dancer took it for granted that her body was a reliable instrument, that it had its own unconscious "wisdom," and that as long as she could do the work for which she was trained, her mode of balance was adequate.

BODY WISDOM

One of the legacies of the last century, with its accent on the God-given perfection of the human frame, was what W. B. Cannon later called "the wisdom of the body."[4] Cannon suggested that there are certain balanced states of the body which are natural and normal and to which, in its wisdom, the body will return after disturbance and stress. Such "body wisdom" was said to apply not only to muscular balance but to the organic constituents of the body. Illness, in this analysis, is accompanied by states of imbalance—the sugar in the blood is constantly raised, the bowel constantly overfull, the vital capacity of the lungs constantly diminished. In this view, the physiological wisdom of the body has to be restored by appropriate medical treatment and care until a more normal resting balance can be maintained —with or without drugs. More and more drugs begin to be needed to keep the blood pressure down, the heartbeat regular, the sleep pattern tolerable. A mental "resting state of balance" is likewise to be achieved by more and more drugs to stop anxiety and depression, or else by the cultivation of a Nirvana state through meditation or other spiritual disciplines.

It is now clear that the "wisdom of the body" theory is a fallacy. Increasing dependence on therapeutic drugs—however wisely and cleverly they may be prescribed—is proof that most people's body wisdom has gone astray.

Nowhere is this clearer than in the muscular-balancing mechanisms which underlie USE. In recent years, popular books like Desmond Morris's *The Naked Ape* have made people aware of the mechanical problems that the upright posture produces.[5] Many nineteenth-century anatomists had assigned varying importance to the upright posture and its accompanying blessings. Some of them customarily saw something partially divine in being upright—"that majestic attitude which announced man's superiority over all the inhabitants of the globe." The naked angel, in fact, rather than the naked ape.

In the first quarter of this century, it was still thought that our spines were perfectly fashioned for the upright posture, but that the world we lived in was to blame. Sir Arthur Keith, who was the authority on posture in the 1920s, thought that postural defects were caused by "the monotonous and trying positions which are entailed by modern education and modern industry."[6]

But in the second quarter of this century, the new specialty of orthopedics came increasingly to the view that it was not man's environment but his imperfect adaptation to it that was at fault. Man was increasingly regarded as a made-over animal, with muscles forced by the adoption of unnatural stances to suffer enormous inequalities in the distribution of labor.[7]

In the second half of this century, a new specialty called ergonomics turned its gaze on how to fit machines to man and man to machines. Chairs, car seats, beds, desks, and all sorts of complex machinery have been designed to give elbowroom and leg length, to give better positioning of pedals, levers, display panels, and proper seat dimensions.

It was hoped thereby to minimize the fatigue and strain of unnecessary movement in faulty positions.

However, because of an inadequate concept of muscular balance, the ergonomic approach has not been really effective. The workingman still arrives home fatigued. Pain in the back affects most of the population, often with crippling severity. In England, 75% of our dentists develop troublesome back pain, and over 80% of our secretaries develop headaches. They have not been helped very much by better-designed equipment. It is their USE which needs redesigning.

Posture both in the home and in the work place is as poor as it ever was—and indeed my figures for adolescents show a deterioration over the past twenty years. Even in the most perfect environment which the ergonomists can construct, the "wisdom of the body" cannot apparently resolve the conflict between those parts of the body which are needed for doing the actual job and those parts which are needed to support the general functioning of the body. Mis-use, in our time, persists and increases.

LIVING ANATOMY

This lack of an adequate concept of muscle balance came originally from the dissecting room. Anatomy, as studied in the corpse, does not bring out the complexity of muscular mis-use in the living man.

The identical sameness of the muscles of any man and woman can indeed be demonstrated in the dissecting room without a shadow of doubt, and students can learn in great detail the names and actions of hundreds of muscles which pull on various levers throughout the body. But this is the anatomy of the dead, the anatomy of sameness.

A living anatomy has to start with the living body and

with the infinite variety of each of us. To give them their due, the ergonomists have always understood the need to study muscle action in the living. Unfortunately they took *mis-used* man as their norm, and much of the equipment which they designed was designed for mis-used man. Only rarely did such equipment encourage really good use, and then only in a most superficial sense. The typist may sit in the statistically perfect chair, but her basic habits of mis-use still persist.

The early anatomists and ergonomists have set the stage for a real understanding of the problem. We now know that man's body is not majestically divine. The "naked ape" has replaced Rousseau's "noble savage" and Wordsworth's "nature's priest." We now know that we are faced with an evolutionary problem of combining the potentiality of an intelligent angel with the impulses of an irascible ape.

Alexander, born just before the last quarter of the nineteenth century, was plunged straight into this evolutionary argument. When Darwin and Huxley made their onslaught on the Book of Genesis, their evolutionary man had still to compete with the image of the divinely created man. He could not be allowed the simple animality of the ape, but he had to have a splendor and grace of his own. His body had to have a natural goodness and wisdom. In this way, Wordsworth's "nature's priest" ("who by the vision splendid, was on his way attended") could hold his head high in competition with the divine image.

It is interesting that Alexander's first book was entitled *Man's Supreme Inheritance.* He was inevitably caught up with the notion of a basic perfection that is lost by a combination of environmental stress and personal stupidity. His whole theme during his lifetime was of an endowment of properly functioning reflexes that the corporeal sin of mis-use, induced by the overstimulating newness of the environment, had clouded over. In this view, a system of

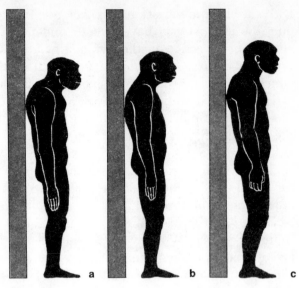

figure 12

perfectly adequate reflexes had to be restored by learning to inhibit wrongly acquired conditioned reflexes. Or, in the words of a recent cleric, by blocking off "ugly contradictions in the true nature of man."

The "vision splendid" has now no need to postulate the perfect God-given or gene-given templet—one correct shape, and one only which is appropriate for our human stance. We have no "true nature," beset with ugly contradictions. To know and to be what we "truly" are, we have to *find out* what we are, and we have to construct what we are to be.

The Alexander Principle suggests that by getting our USE in the right order there is a chance of a new personal evolution. There is no reason to suppose that we are born with a perfectly ordered set of pre-existent natural reflex patterns, and that by refraining from interfering with them all will be as well as it can be. The next step in our evolu-

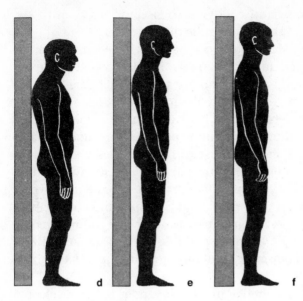

tion has to be learned by each one of us. *Personal selection has to replace natural selection.*

THE UPRIGHT BALANCE

The earliest manlike creatures had a short neck and a well-developed hump. Fig. 12 shows diagrammatically the evolution from (a) Proconsul man, 2,000,000 years ago, to (b) Peking man, 500,000 years ago, to (c) Neanderthal man, 100,000 years ago, to (d) Mount Carmel man, 40,000 years ago, via (e) Modern man, to what I might perhaps call (f) Alexander man! One of the most striking features is the way in which the neck is gradually lengthened and the hump has become less prominent. In the process, the center of gravity has come back, and the point of skull-balance (the occipital condyles) has come back, until the body's center of gravity now falls through this point.

As a result, Modern man's neck has become freer to move; but unfortunately a freely moving neck, although giving him a wide-ranging ability to turn his gaze and his sensory attention around and about himself, also allows him to collapse the vertebrae of his neck and his spine. While a longer neck allows him more potential freedom, it also allows him to use certain muscles for activities and postures in which they should play no part. Speaking, swallowing, and even ordinary breathing are often made to involve muscle groups in the neck and hump which contribute nothing to the act being performed. The more flexible balance that should be made possible is often not actualized. Instead, the potentially free muscles are held fixed in a mis-used balance.

The first thing to notice in the Alexander balance selected for promoting the most efficient functioning (Fig. 5f) is that, compared with Modern man (Fig. 12e), the whole vertebral column is carried much farther back. A plumb line from the mastoid process falls through the trochanter of the thighbone and slightly behind the malleolus of the ankle. Instead of the neck vertebrae and lumbar vertebrae dropping forward and downward, they are directed up and back, not to the point where they are overstrained, but to a point at which excessive muscle tension in the neck and lower back is released. The effect of this is to increase a person's height slightly in younger people, and considerably in older people, who often have shrunk two inches from their younger height by the time they are fifty.

It will also be noticed that the knees are held slightly flexed and the pelvis released, so that the pubis points more toward the front. The sexual organs, instead of being pointed to the floor, with associated buttock tension (the "frozen pelvis"), are presented slightly forward—not by swaying the pelvis forward, but by tipping the pelvis a little on the lumbar spine.

In this balance, the surfaces of the vertebral joints tend to separate rather than to be contracted toward each other. Indeed, the Alexander balance throughout the rest of the body—shoulder blades, shoulders, elbows and hands, hips, knees, ankles and feet—seeks to establish a resting position

11. (a.) Note tension in neck, shoulders, and buttocks.
(b.) Less tension throughout.

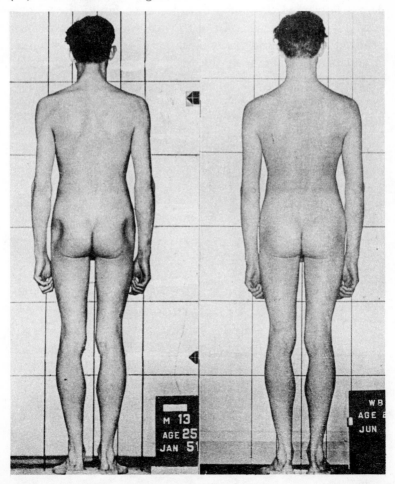

in which all the joint surfaces are not contracted together but are lengthening away from each other. Since neurophysiologists know now that muscle balance is directly related to the *lengthening* of muscle, a new "wisdom of the body" is likely to be facilitated by this lengthening.

Plate 11 shows a patient who suffered from tension headaches: it shows him before and after he had learned to apply the Alexander Principle. Plates 11a and 11b show him photographed from the back view. The most obvious change is that he is taller; and he is wider across the shoulders. Contracted shortened muscles have lengthened.

In Plate 11a, his weight is thrown forward: his neck is dropped forward and his back is arched. Observe the lines of muscle contraction at the back of his neck: the raised

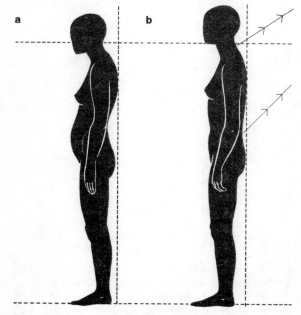

figure 13

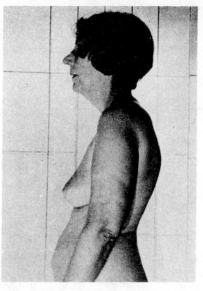

12. Hump in middle-aged woman.

tensed shoulders and the tightened buttocks with exaggerated dimpling. Plate 11b shows him when he has learned to lengthen the contracted neck muscles and to widen the shoulders apart. His buttocks are now uncontracted and he is appreciably taller. And free from tension headaches.

Fig. 13a makes these points diagrammatically. The neck in 13a is dropped down and forward, the back is arched, the pelvis is tipped so that the abdominal contents fall forward. In 13b, the direction of the lengthening has been sketched in. The lines are *up* and *back*, both in the neck and in the lower spine. The head is not pulled backward and down into the chest; the shoulders are not hunched.

Plate 12 shows a typical middle-aged sedentary woman. The neck is dropped forward. The back arches, the pelvis tips forward. The French word for the pelvis—*bassin*—should remind us that it is shaped to contain the abdominal contents, not to let them slop forward over the front of the *bassin*.

SITTING BALANCE

The same principles apply to the sitting position. It was noticed in the last chapter that when most people sit down they contract the head into the shoulders, and as they descend, they usually arch the back and thrust their bottoms out. There is, of course, the alternative method of hurling the body precipitately into an easy chair, with the back flexed into a round ball so that the buttocks land on the front of the seat and the backbone curves along the rest of the seat and up the back of it.

Notice what happens when you sit down slowly. When the heels are apart from each other and the toes turned

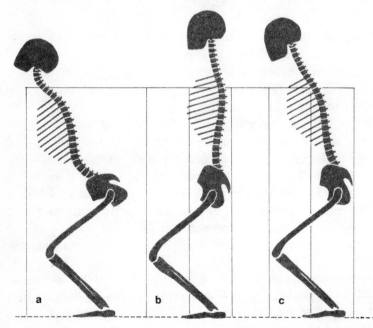

figure 14

out, the kneecap should move continuously forward over the line of the foot (pointing approximately between the big toe and the second toe). As the knees move forward, the body will begin to descend.

At this point (Plate 1), most people will: (a) pull the head back (as in Fig. 2c); (b) throw the lower chest forward; and (c) throw the pelvis backward.

Instead, the body should descend between two vertical lines (Fig. 14b). The pelvis should not push back and the lower chest should not push forward.

Depending on the height of the chair, the vertical axis of the body can then move backward in space. Most people at this point fear that they will lose their balance and fall backward if they continue on downward. This, however, will not happen, provided that the head is not allowed to tighten back. Instead, it must be directed forward at the top of the neck. When the USE is very wrong, it may be necessary (Fig. 14c) to bend slightly forward at the hip joint.

For most people this is not easy at first, except perhaps in drama and movement colleges, where they have to think about body mechanics in detail.

If the head is constantly drawn back into the shoulders when you are sitting down, you will arrive in a wrong seated position in which the head is hunched into the shoulders. This will lead to hump formation and the associated muscle tension and mis-use it implies. By moving in this way, the spine gradually becomes shortened, like a string of beads (Fig. 15a) which is straight when lengthened but goes into curves when it is shortened (Fig. 15b).

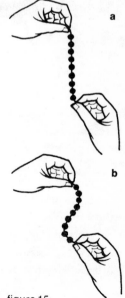

figure 15

HEAD BALANCE

It should not be thought that the Alexander head balance is simply a matter of idiosyncratic choice. There can be few anatomists and physiologists who do not now accept—in theory, at least—the importance of head position. The general reader may be interested to know a little about the vestibular apparatus in the inner ear, which gives us much information about our balance and about variations in pressures that act on our bodies.

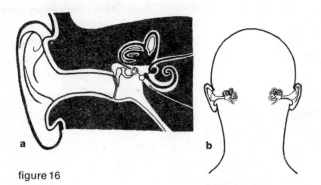

figure 16

The vestibular apparatus (Fig. 16) lies inside the skull, internal to the mastoid process, and it registers variations in pressure both from outside and from inside the body. When we stop or start moving, when we lean on things, or when we fix one part of our body closer to another part, this apparatus should help to tell us what is happening. In like manner, it gives us information about our spatial orientation and about the way we are supporting our body against gravity on various surfaces—our feet on the ground, our buttocks on a seat, our back when we are lying down.

It does this by means of built-in spirit levels (Fig. 16b)—the so-called labyrinth. The names of the particular parts do not matter; the essence of their function is that there are cavities placed at right angles in three planes in the skull which are filled with a heavy gelatinous fluid, and in contact with this fluid there are a number of hairs projecting from the cavity walls.

The weight of the fluid drags on the hairs in accordance with the head position, and as we move or rotate our bodies, the inertia of the fluid jogs it up and down against the hairs. The cavities also have a small flap—a "cupola"—which sways like a swing door to and from a resting position. All of this sends information to the brain about body positionings in the vertical and longitudinal axes—up/down, right/left, front/back—and it also gives information about acceleration and deceleration, by displacement of the gelatinous fluid. It does this more accurately if it is carried on a symmetrically balanced head.

The skull, carrying the eyes as well as the vestibular apparatus, gives a sense of position and acceleration. In modern civilization, the eyes are frequently being dropped to read or to write or to perform manual tasks. Dropping of the eyes very soon involves a habit of dropping the head forward from the hump, a position that may be held for long periods. As a result, when the eyes are raised, the tendency is for the head to pull back at the point where the neck joins the skull, thus perpetuating the hump and further encouraging the head to be held retracted at the top of the neck.

A correct resting head balance, in which the vestibular apparatus can be carried on an even keel, provides a stable platform from which the special senses—eyes, mouth, nose, and ears—can work. All too often, the vestibular apparatus sacrifices its primary position to the demands of the other senses—the eyes to focus on (or reject) certain sights, the ears to pick up (or block out) certain sounds, etc. Our precariously evolved head balance is easily disturbed by the bombardments of the modern world and by our incessant desire to pick up or reject information through our special senses. It becomes a prime necessity that we should re-establish a balanced resting position for the head.

SLUMP

Alexander USE suggests, then, that if adequate functioning is to be maintained the head balance should not be upset, and it follows from this that the back should not be allowed to slump when sitting (Plate 13a). Many people at first find it hard to maintain a lengthening balance when they are seated. Lengthening (Plate 13b, Fig. 13b) is often wrongly interpreted as the need to sit up overstraight, with the back arched and the chest pushed out, and with the weight carried through the upper thigh instead of through the ischial tuberosities—the two small knuckles of bone at the back of the pelvis. Yet in fact the lengthening position (Plate 13c) is restful and efficient, and soon comes to feel comfortable, once the habit has been acquired.

Not only when you are sitting up straight, but when you are leaning forward to eat, to write, or to read, the back should not be collapsed forward from the hump but should be pivoted forward from the hip joints so that the pelvis is integrated with the rest of the back. In this way, there will be no excessive slumping in the lower back and the whole trunk will not collapse forward.

In addition to the lengthened use of the trunk, the knees, as I have already said, should never be crossed when sitting. Whenever it is socially possible and there is enough room, the knees should be pointed away from each other. In particular, most forms of lower back pain will be benefited by

directing the knees away from each other. This applies
especially to sedentary workers, who sit at desks all day
long.

Once you sit down, it is usually best to move your pelvis
right to the back of the chair seat, and this applies to almost
all seats—cinema, bus, and train seats, dining chairs, and
easy chairs—whenever the leg length allows it. Unfortunately many modern chairs—particularly those with a

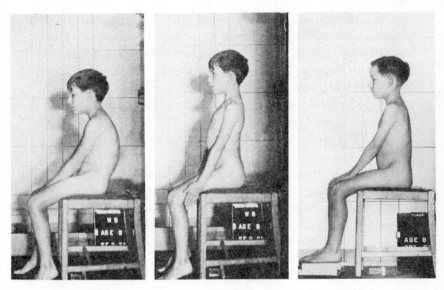

13. (a.) Slumping.   (b.) Sitting too straight. (c.) Balanced.

marked curve between the upright and the horizontal—
make good USE almost impossible. Much leisure seating
needs redesigning.

The television habit has led to a great deterioration in
children's sitting posture. Television, whether we like it or
not, is with us to stay, in one form or another. It should
not be too difficult for parents to encourage their children

not to collapse and slump as they watch the screen. If children are too tired for this—after school, for example—it is best to arrange for them to lie down with their backs supported rather than to sit slumping.

Children, when shown, are able to maintain the balance I have been describing without strain and effort, and they become less tired by their schoolwork as a result. Forces in their environment do, however, conspire to teach them to mis-use their bodies as discussed in Chapter 2.

Alexander balance may at first sound as if it entails an immense effort. The learning of it when it has been lost will certainly entail effort, but when it is learned, most people find it feels so good and easy that they would not willingly throw it away.

BALANCED WISDOM

Not only is man poorly designed for achieving balance—poor in the sense that it does not come easily and automatically to us—but also there has been little instruction in how to get the best out of our particular model. Secretaries and car drivers have had plenty of scientific investigation into the design of their desks and chairs and their car seats. Like the rest of us, they are expected to know how to make the best they can out of the body work provided by their parents. Even though a muscular body is looked upon with a certain amount of envy, we have not yet learned to recognize the importance of a properly balanced pelvis or a sensibly placed sacrum. It may be appreciated that the dressage rider needs to sit so that he can control his horse through the sensitivity of his buttock adjustment; but a sensitively poised sitting position to be used in the idle boredom of an office or to replace the stupefying collapse of politicians on their parliamentary benches and in their committees has not yet received the attention it deserves. When they are sitting, even the most famous of athletes do not seem immune from a state of collapse that ages them prematurely and eventually nullifies their potentialities.

Posture

Unfortunately a serious imbalance may not affect biological functioning in an obvious way at first, and this accounts for the bizarre variations in posture which come to be accepted as normal and suitable for particular social situations and surroundings.

There is no one single social criterion of good posture. The barrack-square sergeant, the nurse, the anthropologist, the dancer, the gynecologist, the sculptor, the actor, the Buddhist monk—these and many more will all have their particular ideas of what is right. The adolescent thinks it essential to adopt the typical slouch; the model shows off her clothes with grotesquely thrown-forward pelvis; the shop assistant and the bar drinker relax with weight on one leg; the professional beauty queen arches her back and pushes out her bosom—and so on, through the whole range of body language that we may think suitable and appropriate. None of these postures would matter too much if their perpetrators had some idea of a postural norm to which they could return when the immediate pressure of the social moment was over. But these distortions *become* each person's own norm, and feel so right that a properly balanced use of the body soon feels unnatural. Momentary attitudes in time change to habitual dispositions. The body is soon molded into fixed patterns which to a large extent will determine future performance and future functioning.

Clearly, we cannot rely on a *social* criterion of what constitutes good USE. *It is from their effect on biological functioning that the variety of body uses must be judged.*

There are many alternative possibilities in the mechanical use of the body at any given time, but for any given situation there is a way of using the body that makes for the best functioning with the least wear and tear.

Many writers before Alexander have written of this need for ease and economy of effort. Schopenhauer considered that the USE was good if every movement was performed and every position assumed in the easiest, most appropriate, and convenient way—"the pure adequate expression of intention without any superfluity which might exhibit itself in aimless meaningless bustle."[8] Unfortunately the "easiest and most convenient way," although perhaps socially appropriate and convenient, is not necessarily biologically appropriate. Herbert Spencer perhaps came nearer to it when he spoke of "movements which are effected with economy of force, and postures which are maintained within this economy."[9] Similarly, Marcus Aurelius wrote, "The body ought to be stable and free from all irregularity whether in rest or in motion. All this should be without any element of affectation." Thomas Aquinas thought that good use consisted in "due proportion, for the sense delights in things duly proportioned: delight springs from evidence of ease in the performer."[10]

But what is easeful USE? When mis-use patterns are never relinquished, but are present even at rest, we are confronted with a state of pervading disease and strain that stops life from being lived as it should be. The fact is that the majority of people do not really know how to achieve an easeful state of rest in their bodies. When their childhood remedy of a good night's sleep fails to restore them to full enjoyable energy, they seek for artificial sleep and artificial tension release; and the drugs they use produce a state of dullness that is a mockery of what living should be.

Dystonia

Dystonic patterns, the medical name for faulty muscular tension patterns, arise and produce an unbalanced resting state in many ways. They are particularly obvious in the positionings and postures that we adopt when we are keeping still. Over one thousand such body positions have been listed, all variations of sitting and lying and standing and kneeling. Some of them seem unusual to Western eyes, but the deep squat (Fig. 17a) and the tailor squat (Fig. 17c) employ a far better use of the back than, say, the familiar adolescent postures of Fig. 17d and Fig. 17f. Fig. 17e, in which the legs are not crossed, is functionally far better than the familiar crossed-knee position of Fig. 17b.

Dystonic patterns will also arise in the simple mechanical

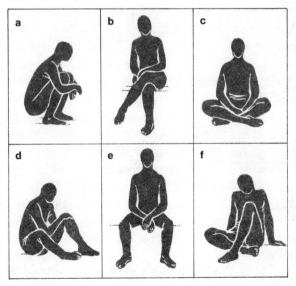

figure 17

actions which we carry out all day as we move ourselves and objects in our surroundings—moving a fork; moving a book, a paper, a telephone; moving a dishcloth, an oven door, an electric switch; moving a gear handle, a coin, a bus ticket —the list is endless. Dystonic mis-uses appear when we walk and run, jump, hurdle, swim, throw, dance; when we swing a golf club, a tennis racket, a cricket bat, a conductor's baton; when we ride on a horse, a bus, or a bicycle; when we sit slumped in a dinghy or huddled over a textbook in the library; when we lift a dish or a dictionary from a shelf; when we stand at a bar or in a shop or at a football match; when we carry out surgical operations or laboratory work or dentistry; when we work manually in industry or agriculture or just in the garden. Our performance and our liability to fatigue are bound to be influenced by our manner of use. There are many ways of using the body—some carry short-term advantages but long-term disadvantages. The seamstress and the racing cyclist eventually have to pay for their crouching posture.

In activities that need a special skill, muscular dystonia leads to unpredictability of performance. To consider only one athletic sphere, many of our top-class women tennis players in Britain never seem quite to live up to their earlier promise. They may have some isolated successes, but often, just when their biggest opportunity comes, they become suddenly erratic. Most of them show marked dystonic patterns around the shoulders, upper back, and neck that are accentuated as they come under pressure. As the game proceeds, they are seen not to relax their tension, and they do not come back to a proper resting balance. They visibly begin moving into their strokes by a mis-use of their neck and shoulders.

Of course, in the midst of a game—or indeed of any intense activity—there has to be an orientation to and a concentration of effort and expectancy on the matter in hand. But apart from the arts and certain forms of interpersonal gamesmanship, we are faced with two questions: how are we not to mis-use our bodies when we start to do something, and when we stop, how are we to release the muscular contractions which we have just been making?

Such a muscular control will become possible only if we can start from a properly balanced state of rest, and if we know how to return to (and maintain) a steady state of muscular rest when we stop.

Postural Homeostasis

About twenty years ago, I suggested the phrase "postural homeostasis" to describe the steady state in which the body keeps itself balanced. "Stasis" means "pertaining to bodies at rest and in equilibrium." "Homeostasis" means how we adjust ourselves to maintain balance. Postural homeostasis involves a most intricate and delicate interplay of muscular coordinations and adjustments throughout the body, to bring the body close to a balanced state.

The balance that results from this interplay is in what the physicists call "a steady resting state." In a healthy person these muscular adjustments will mesh together to give a balanced whole: a juggler who balances a number of objects on a pole is maintaining them in a "steady resting state." Work is being done to maintain balance around a central point of stillness. This central point is not fixed. Oscillation takes place around it, with smaller or larger swings.

Such oscillation is characteristic of all our muscular activities. If you look at yourself in a mirror, you will see that you are swaying slightly. If you place a piece of string down the mirror, stand back about ten feet, and line up your nose with the piece of string, you will notice that as you walk toward the mirror your nose oscillates a great deal from one side of the string to the other.

Even when you stand still, a pinpoint of light photographed on the top of your skull would show a great deal of sway around the central point. H. J. Eysenck has confirmed that in neurotic people such swaying oscillations are much larger than in healthy people.[11] Indeed, the amount of sway is one of the clearest indications of conflict in people's personalities. Balance can be achieved in all manner of ways. Many of these ways are markedly inefficient, with too big an oscillation away from the central resting point.

Muscular Feedback

What governs the amount of oscillation (disturbance) in our muscular adjustments? Think of a simple movement like moving the tip of the right index finger (X) to touch the tip of your nose (Y). The distance between X and Y has to be assessed by our brain rather in the way a cat gauges how to jump from a window ledge (X) to a parapet (Y).

The distance between X and Y is known in cybernetic jargon as the "error." Information about the "error" XY is fed back to the brain, where it is unconsciously checked against a pre-existing model (the receptor element in the diagram below). According to the construction we place upon the information received, action takes place in the muscles (the effector element M, in the diagram) to move from X to Y. In other words, to close the gap and eliminate the error.

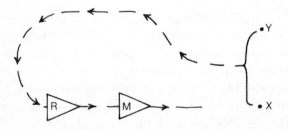

This diagram is the prototype of a homeostatic circuit, and it involves what is known as "negative feedback." Negative feedback keeps a system oscillating very close to a central resting state, and when there is too big a movement away from the resting position, it brings it back by a compensatory movement. The receptor element R represents our idea of what—for one reason or another—we consider to be a normal resting state. Through it, we receive information and compute it against our previously stored experience. We all have a "body-construct," made up of all the previously learned experience of our body, and we construe (put a construction on) what happens to us by reference to this "body-construct."

We can think of "error" as being the difference between the way we construe things to be and the way we want them to be. And, of course, we all of us construe things—and alter our perception of them—to make them seem the way we want them to be.

The feedback circuit in the diagram is similar to the scanning mechanism that is used in television and radar. The muscles are scanned as one might scan a printed page in search for a word. A thermostat is another example: when it corrects an error, it makes a new one; it further corrects this by making a smaller one. It is in fact in a state of "steady motion." When the self-correcting mechanism overshoots the mark, oscillation will occur.

Riding a bicycle is another example. When the rider falls slightly to the right, he turns his front wheel to the right, which stops his fall but leads to his being thrown to the left, and he corrects this by turning his wheel to the left, and so on. The net result is a steady resting state in his body as he uses his arms and his legs to steer and to pedal.

If our USE is to be accurately balanced, at least four things are needed. We need to get adequate information from our muscles (and from the other parts concerned with movement). We need to receive this information accurately in our brain without obscuring it. We need to activate our muscles so that they do what we want with a minimum of mis-use. We need to know how to come back to—and maintain—a balanced resting use of our bodies that will interfere least with our functioning.

Muscle Physiology

In a book of this nature, it is impossible to give a full account of all that is relevant in muscle physiology. The already complex study of nerve and muscle has become yearly more complex. Except at a fairly crude level of neuromuscular injury or pathology, it is still almost impossible to relate either the old or the new muscle physiology to what actually happens to "normal" human beings at rest and in movement. I know of no other sphere of physiology in which acutely intelligent minds have labored with such imagination and skill—Sherrington, Eccles, Denny-Brown, Matthews, Granit, etc. Most of the best aspects of biological research seem to find their expression in this particular discipline. Yet in spite of all this fine physiological work and speculation, the task of teaching muscular control to people in their actual daily affairs has not yet been greatly facilitated by it.

Muscle can either shorten or lengthen. It contracts by means of a molecular shortening, which pulls on elastic elements in the muscle fibers, and the contraction is produced by nerve impulses—increased, damped down, held in check, explosively poured out, synchronized, or facilitated by numerous relay stations in the brain and spinal cord. Eventually the resultant impulse to a muscle fiber, delivered at a certain intensity to a muscle in a more or less receptive state, makes it contract—i.e., shorten.

We have two systems (Fig. 18) by which our muscles are controlled by motor nerves (i.e., nerves that go to the muscle

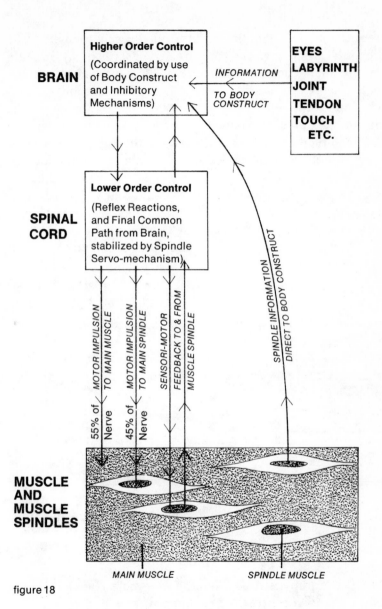

figure 18

from the brain). The first, and until recently thought to be the only, system works, as already described, by making muscle fibers contract and shorten. Fifty-five percent of the motor nerves look after this activity. The second system, which uses the remaining 45% of the motor nerves, works on quite a different basis. The nerves from this system do not go directly to actual muscle—to the biceps muscle or thigh muscle which you can touch with your hand—but to a complex structure, called a muscle spindle, lying within the belly of the anatomical muscles. Many, many thousands of these lie lengthways in the muscles. They are about 8 mm long, bulging in the middle, and tapered at the ends. They are concerned with the lengthening of muscle, and not with its contraction.

The muscle spindle has its own set of internal striated

14. Muscle spindle lengthwise (*top*). Cut through vertically (*below*) to show small internal muscles and large external muscles.

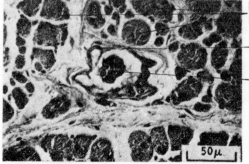

muscles (Plate 14), and in addition to the motor nerves that go to it from the brain and spinal cord it has sensory nerves that go from it back to the brain and spinal cord. The spindle is a much more sensitive adjuster of muscle than is the overlying anatomical muscle itself. Its register of length works in parallel with the overlying muscle, not only to damp down excessive oscillations during activity but also to induce a lengthening of contracted muscle after activity. In the words of P. A. Merton, it "constitutes a follow-up servo, the muscle length tending to follow changes in spindle length. . . ." (*British Medical Bulletin* 12:214-218).

The whole mechanism is extremely complex, but from the point of view of someone who is attempting to learn a properly balanced use of his body, two major points arise: first, the overcontraction and shortening of anatomical muscle may result in the muscle spindle going silent (i.e., failing to feed back information to the brain about how much the muscles are contracting). A spindle stops discharging when overshortening of the main muscle occurs. And second, the lengthening of anatomical muscles can be brought about not simply by stopping off the activity which originally made that muscle contract, *but by learning voluntarily to lengthen muscles until they achieve a better resting length.*

Apparently the muscle spindle plays a very large part in this production of length in contracted muscle. It should be mentioned that spindles are connected not only with the cerebral cortex (through which we control our actions) but with the reticular formation (the nerve network in our brain that is responsible for our conscious awareness of the world about us and our ability to think about and react to it).

We can consciously learn to lengthen tense muscles not just by stopping the action that made them contract but as a definite act of will by which we can release and relengthen contracted muscle.

This, of course, is a simplified account, and it must be, since any nervous pathway we can trace in the brain ultimately connects up, directly or indirectly, with muscles or muscle spindles. Any frequently repeated use of a particular nervous pathway is likely to lead to the slow development of a "cell assembly"—a diffuse structure of cells in the cortex and midbrain and basal ganglia capable of acting as an enclosed "memory" system that influences other systems and is influenced by other systems. The cross-correlations of motor and sensory nerves, to and from a vast number of units, and spindles in a large number of muscles, via the spinal cord and all levels of the brain, are fully described in textbooks.

No doubt the Alexander Principle will before long be greatly clarified and refined by new paradigms of associative mechanisms in perception, but meanwhile the practical business of detecting and re-educating faulty use patterns can proceed quite satisfactorily with the simplified view I am suggesting.

Faulty Resting Balance

The patient in Plate 15a shows a dystonic pattern both when she is standing upright and when she sits down (15b). The slight twist of her pelvis to the right when she stands becomes much greater when she sits down, and it can can be seen that when she sits down she makes an excessive muscle contraction on the left side of her back (just above her pants) which is an accentuation of a similar contraction when she is standing.

Such muscle patterns can be recorded electrically. Fig. 19 is an electromyographic recording that I published some years ago in the *Lancet* (1955, 2:659). In 19a, the left side of the back shows considerably more activity than the right.

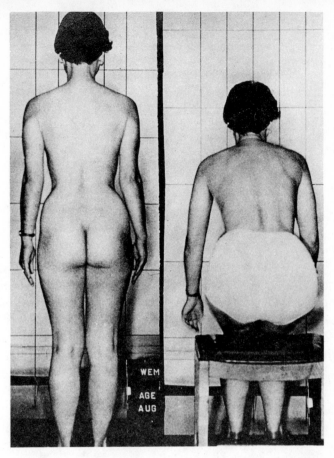

15. Note: neck tension at back, raised right shoulder, tension on left side of lower back, pelvis twisting to right.

In 19b, when she is moving, there is activity on both sides of the back but more in the left. Her back, in fact, shows a dystonic pattern that distorts the posture of the back and, in her case, produced pressure on one of her lumbar disks. But, in addition, her resting position was an unbalanced position. Her balance around a central resting point showed excessive oscillations, because of the asymmetry in her muscular resting position.

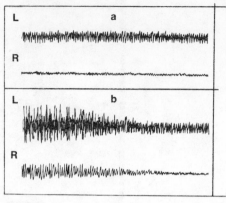

figure 19

Fig. 20 is a recording of the neck muscles of a violinist who consulted me because he suffered painful cramps at the base of his neck when he was playing fast passages. In Fig. 20a the muscle is relatively quiet. In Fig. 20b he picks up his bow and puts it down. In Fig. 20c he again picks it

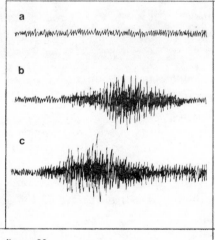

figure 20

up and puts it down, but this time the muscle continues to be in a state of activity even when he is doing nothing. His feedback mechanism has gone wrong, and at this point he has no idea of how to release the contraction, but has to rely on its eventually subsiding—an impossibility while he is giving a concert. It is clear that he needs to be taught how to return at will to a properly balanced resting state.

As a simple illustration of the resting-state principle— a knee-jerk hammer (Fig. 21a), which has a heavy head on a flexible wooden handle, will, if agitated, oscillate around a resting point (Fig. 21b). Application of an external force (Fig. 21c) will deform it, and after removal of this force, it will either return to its original resting state

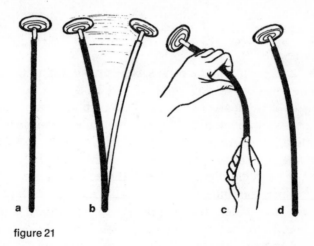

figure 21

or it will remain to a greater or lesser degree deformed (Fig. 21d). In time, repeated application of such a force will lead to structural alteration or, at any rate, to a predisposition to bend more easily, just as a paper, once folded, tends to bend more easily in the folded direction.

Dystonic mis-use is present when we do not know how to

return to a balanced resting state after reacting to a given situation. Such overactive states in time become habitual, and a predisposition to adopt them will persist even when, owing to a different muscular organization being evoked by a new situation, they temporarily disappear.

In time, not only does the resting state of the muscle become incorrectly balanced, but it begins to modify the bones and joints on which it works and also the circulatory system that traverses it. The bony framework becomes warped and cramped and stretched by the stresses and strains that are put on it by persistent overcontraction of muscle. These states of overcontraction, large and small, gradually leave their mark on us until our resting state is in its various ways as deformed as the patella hammer in Fig. 21.

Relaxation

There have been many recipes for getting rid of such unwelcome tension. Most people can get by for quite long periods by one means or another, even though they already show persistent dystonia. At the same time, most people, by the time adolescence is over, if not before, begin to feel that something is amiss, and they may already be showing mental or physical disturbances that either create symptoms or impair performance.

As we grow older, the resting state that we all learn to adopt is either a balanced or an unbalanced one, according to the degree of maldistributed muscle tension. Muscular hypertension is the residual tension and postural deformity that remain after stress activity—or after any activity that leaves behind residual muscle tension. Such residual tension can be resolved by returning to a balanced resting state, or it can be partially relaxed or diminished by various other means, without, however, the actual pattern being resolved.

In the latter case, the tension will remain latent in an un-balanced resting state, so that it may require only the idea of moving to reactivate the muscular hypertension, usually in the form of anticipatory tension or "set."

Two alternatives therefore are possible. First, the tension can be relaxed a little without resolving the underlying dystonic pattern, which remains latent until the conditions for its renewal occur. Second—and this is what is needed—the tension can be resolved by return to a balanced resting state, leaving no unconscious residue.

Most people don't understand what a balanced resting state entails. With or without the help of their doctor, they resort to the first procedure. Under such titles as "relaxation," "rest cure," "tranquilizing," or simply by such expedients as alcohol, nicotine, and slump-collapse at weekends, a temporary diminution of disagreeable tension may be obtained. If these people avoid the stress situation or the memory of it, they may discover a sufficient number of "funk holes" by which they can avoid activation of the latent tension. The resultant lack of vitality, creativity, and enjoyment of forward planning (which would activate the tension state) eventually becomes the normal way such people spend their lives.

A balanced resting state is not so difficult to attain, but there is widespread ignorance of what it entails. When someone is in a tension state, there is fear of return to a state of rest, since this would involve the realization of a "true" emotional experience, and a truer self-picture. Our preferred self-picture is usually sustained by using ourselves in a habitual way. By maintaining an unbalanced USE, we can maintain self-deception and escape the truer picture of ourselves that would become apparent in a balanced resting state of USE.

CHAPTER 4

Use and Disease

MEDICAL DIAGNOSIS

The whole world of medicine and disease is fraught with fear. The television revolution may have taught us that doctors are fallible human beings, but in moments of dire need the patient's fear of illness and pain causes him to invest his doctor with superhuman faculties and wisdom. The patient who is unable to pass water and whose full bladder is making him scream with agony would at that moment give much of his personal fortune to someone who could relieve him. Most doctors will have experienced from such patients a depth of gratitude that affirms them in a view of themselves as basically useful people.

The doctor, with his *therapeutic* skill, will always be loved, feared, and respected. But such rewarding moments of therapy do not happen very often. A vast amount of general medical practice is concerned with humdrum palliative measures, with relatively dissatisfied and grumbling sick people, and with a mixture of kindness and counseling, or, in bad doctors, of brusqueness and dogmatism. Patients in these circumstances tend to be labeled with a convenient diagnosis.

Hospital practice also has its rewarding moments of therapeutic skill—in the accident wards, in the labor wards, in the intensive care units, and sometimes in the skillful handling of modern drugs that can stem acute infection and acute depression. But much of the hospital doctor's time is spent in bowing down to the great god Diagnosis. To understand the connection between USE and disease, it is necessary to know what is meant by "a diagnosis," and in the process discover what a disease isn't.

When you walk into a doctor's consulting room, he begins right away to label you. At first his labeling is a rough one— you look ill. If he is to decide what sort of "ill" you are, he has to examine a few more of your characteristics.

In all of us at any time there are a vast number of physiological events taking place. The body is a complex whole in a state of perpetual process—a veritable "flux of events." Your doctor would like to know which of these events are not functioning as they should.

The events that contribute to our organized make-up are interdependent, but it is possible to select some of them for measurement. Details of malfunctioning events can then be collected into a "bundle of events." This "bundle" is the diagnosis.

The bundles of events (diagnostic labels), into which individual events (tissue changes and behavioral patterns, etc.) can be grouped, do not exist in the same way that the individual events themselves may be said to exist. The process of bundling together events into diagnostic labels is simply a form of classification adopted from constant usage and embodying the cumulative experience of many doctors. The classifications do not have an independent existence in their own right: they are not there, like the North Pole, waiting to be discovered.

I don't deny the immense usefulness and convenience of a descriptive diagnosis. It is simply that diseases are labels —words. There are no diseases—only sick people. What doctors call diseases are states of functioning of many people, no two alike, but similar enough for general concepts to be formed.

Descriptive Falsification

Before considering how and why USE should be one of the "events" to be considered in making a diagnosis, let us inquire further why an explanatory diagnostic label, as it is used at present, is only of limited value. Consider the case of John G., an insurance broker, aged 42, who was admitted to a hospital in the middle of the night with a gastric ulcer that had perforated. He was already known to the hospital and had been treated there four months previously. I only knew him socially and not in a medical capacity, but it was clear that he was creating a tension state in himself that was certain to produce symptoms again of some kind.

When he had previously been in the hospital with a complaint of abdominal pain, he was fully investigated: a barium meal had shown that an ulcer crater was present in his stomach. The diagnosis "gastric ulcer" was made, and following a period of treatment he lost his pain and returned home. After a short convalescence he returned to work.

Why was such a diagnosis of "gastric ulcer" inadequate, since it was clearly the correct explanation of his pain? Because when we classify the patient as "a case of gastric ulcer," we are referring not merely to the ulcer itself but to the whole patient, his whole history, and his whole personal and social nexus. The patient is not a "gastric ulcer." The diagnosis "gastric ulcer" does not exist in the same way that the observed ulcer crater might be said to exist. The *bundle* of events ("gastric ulcer") is not the same as the individual pathological event (the gastric ulcer crater). The preoccupation with the label and the ulcer crater dominated John G.'s doctors to such an extent that they were content simply to have eradicated the ulcer crater, the pathological explanation of his illness. The fact that John G. broke down again with a perforation four months later shows that the whole concept of diagnosis had slipped up somewhere. It was not enough to have sent him home with a diet and drugs and a diagnosis which explained his ulcer. Indeed, the obsession with explanatory diagnosis is to a certain extent responsible for the impersonal treatment that patients encounter, whether it be in hospital or from their general practitioners. The "patient as a person" is easily lost in a too facile labeling process, by which over-importance is given to the "real" pathological lesion that is needed to explain the illness. What is needed is a diagnosis which can predict to some extent the likely course of an illness, so that we can prescribe appropriately for the future.

We can see from the case of John G. how the word used for a *predictive* diagnostic label is often identical with the word used for an *explanatory* label, and this is usually the name of a specific local lesion or disorder of functioning—"gastric ulcer," or "prolapsed intervertebral disk," or "bronchitis." The muddle arises most insidiously, because the same diagnostic label has to perform these two different roles of explanation and prediction. The muddle is so deep-seated that many doctors feel that it is crazy not to admit that "diabetes" causes a raised blood sugar, or that "bronchitis" causes purulent sputum, or that "depression" causes depression. Yet how can a classification cause anything?

In our language we cannot refer to events which are

going on somewhere without introducing a name, a word, or phrase which appears to stand for something which is producing them. But since most of us still have the primitive belief that to every name an underlying real entity must correspond, it becomes only too easy for the patient to think that a symptom is produced by some underlying "morbid entity," which corresponds to the classificatory label that is used. And while most doctors would reckon to diagnose on the basis of "will it be useful to label it as one," labels have a way of gaining a spurious objectivity, and leading a life of their own.

Of course, at first, the patient and his doctor need a satisfactory explanation of the symptom which is troubling him. If the patient starts vomiting, is it due to the lunchtime oysters or is it due to a brain tumor starting to press on the centers in the brain (to take an extreme example)? When John G. started vomiting up blood in the middle of the night, the likely explanation was his old ulcer crater. So far, so good. The ulcer crater is an event, and correct explanation is always in terms of events—oysters, ulcer craters, intra-cranial pressure. However, once an "event-explanation" has been arrived at, the more difficult matter then arises of constructing the predictive diagnosis which will suggest ways of handling the patient in the future. Explanation and prediction are two quite separate matters.

This means that a predictive label must include more events than those needed for the immediate explanation. Lack of amines in the brain may, of course, sometimes produce depression, but the predictive label "depression" must include many more alterable events than amine lack. Lack of insulin may, of course, produce a high blood sugar, but the predictive label "diabetes" must include more alterable events than insulin lack. Bronchial inflammation (bronchitis) may, of course, produce purulent sputum, but the predictive label "bronchitis" must include many more alterable events than bronchial inflammation. The label "gastric ulcer" must include many more alterable events than the actual gastric ulceration, and so on. A patient's USE is one such event.

We can improve the predictive value of our diagnostic label by learning to include more and more events in the "bundle of events" that makes it up. The events can be collected at all levels from the patient: physical, chemical, bacteriological, cells, tissues, organs, and so on up to the higher mental functions and to his personal and social behavior—behavior that is manifested in his USE. It is not that events at the physical and chemical levels are to be seen as an *explanation* of events at another, "higher" level, but simply that, when we come to apply a *predictive* label, we should make up bundles of events from whatever levels may help us to prescribe future action.

•

DESCRIPTION AND PRESCRIPTION

Habitually wrong USE should always be considered when making a selection of events to be included in the "bundle of events" that makes up a diagnosis. Any diagnosis that has not considered USE is liable to fall down—sometimes to a lesser, usually to a greater degree.

If USE is to be included in the making of a diagnosis, we must realize that a diagnosis should encompass two things. It should contain a *description* and it should contain a *prescription*—a description of events that are malfunctioning and a prescription of principles for future amelioration and prevention.

Diagnosis has for too long looked only for descriptive explanations, whether they be "dispositional" explanations, "efficient cause" explanations, or "final cause" explanations. Such descriptive diagnosis may satisfy the desire for pigeonholing, but it does not necessarily carry implications for long-term prevention. A descriptive diagnosis tends to see the patient in a deterministic manner, at the mercy of his genes, his chemistry, his reflexes, and his social commitments. Patients tend to be seen as objects lacking free will, and not as persons. In the preoccupation with pathological minutiae, the patient as a person is lost.

This "descriptivism" (as it is termed by the philosophers[12]) can, of course, be counterbalanced, and in many doctors it is counterbalanced by art and understanding, but it often happens that doctors have less intuitive understanding than ordinary unschooled people. From his earliest days in the dissecting room, the medical student has to stifle troublesome feelings that may be stirred up by, say, handling a corpse. He soon learns, in this and many other situations, to filter out his ordinary feelings and to lock himself in a scientific enclosure where he denies himself the ordinary reactions of the outside world. By so doing, he is able to see his patients as objects for scientific scrutiny, and not personally in a way that might require overinvolvement. Such an approach may give him confidence and a tranquil mind, but it is confidence purchased at the price of psychological blindness.

This *descriptivism* is naïvely deterministic. It does not take sufficient account of the patient's free will. *Prescriptivism*, on the contrary, says that as long as people are willing to make up their minds about what to do next, they can be free. But in making up their minds about future action, they have to make a prediction about the future—an opinion, a hypothesis, a diagnosis of what seems likely to happen or desirable to make happen. Such a "prescriptive diagnosis" does not imply that all future events are or could be predictable. In the realm of health, it simply seeks to include in its diagnostic bundle events that are likely to affect the patient's health in the future. It seeks not simply to describe the present, but to prescribe action for the future. And it prescribes the action on a basis of principles, of priorities.

The Alexander Principle says that USE will always affect FUNCTIONING. It says that USE should always be included in a prescriptive diagnosis. It says it will always be important for anyone anywhere to know how to sustain a good manner of USE, in sickness or in health. It seeks to replace the concept of *cure* by the concept of *prevention*.

PREVENTIVE MEDICINE

From the patient's point of view, all medicine is preventive medicine—preventing what is feared might happen as well as what is actually happening: preventing pain; preventing a lump from growing and spreading; preventing headache, insomnia, agitation, depression, cough, fatigue, giddiness; stopping overweight, stopping underweight; preventing the hazards of childbirth, preventing even the child being born; preventing the aching back, the tingling fingers, and so on.

Health, for most of us, implies that we are able without strain to do the things we expect to be able to do, and that we are able without strain to be the way we like to be. Restoration to contented functioning is what most people mean by being healthy. When we begin to worry about the presence of possible disease, we are concerned about what may happen next.

The general scientific and technological explosion which got under way in the 1920s has dominated medical thought and training for the past half-century. But the explosion is now becoming a spent force. The gains are immense; the new medical skills and tools have undeniably altered our whole concept of how to deal with severe illness. Many con-

ditions whose progress could not be adequately prevented
before can now be successfully checked.

Most readers know that they have good reason to thank
medicine for taking the terror out of acute illness, but they
also know that it is rare nowadays to find a really healthy
happy human being—and one who sustains his health
over most of a lifetime. They accept the fact that many
symptoms can be managed by the use of powerful psycho-
tropic drugs or by powerful antibiotics, but they are also
aware that medicine has little to offer them in certain other
conditions where their functioning is not as good as they
would like it to be.

There are a large number of major conditions—mental
disorders, rheumatic disorders, and breathing disorders, to
mention only three—in which many patients are greatly
incapacitated in spite of everything that medicine has to
offer.

THE USE DIAGNOSIS

If USE is the single most important factor that remains
to be dealt with by medical science, the reason for the lack
of help a patient gets from the average doctor in certain
cases is apparent. *Doctors—through no fault of their own—
have not been trained to observe in detail the variegated
patterns of mis-use that are going on in all their patients.*

To say this is not to claim that a faulty manner of use is
the main cause of most unexplained malfunctioning—
although in many cases there is a clear causal connection.
While most other types of diseased functioning come under
the scrutiny of the medical eye, USE is generally ignored.
It is not one of the "events" that are considered when
putting together the diagnostic "bundle of events." And
since those whose USE is reasonably good seem to avoid—

or, at least, postpone—many of the ills to which human beings are prone, any diagnosis that does not consider this factor is incomplete. Fundamental to the preventive care of a patient is the teaching of improved habits of life, and this means teaching an improved USE.

Such a conception goes beyond our present regimes of medical attention. It does not in any way preclude the need for accurate pathological descriptive diagnosis, but it does mean that no prescription for treatment is complete until a person's USE has been considered.

Two types of disorder stand at the top of all the illness league tables—mental disorders and rheumatic disorders. If we consider only that part of the population who leave their homes to work (excluding adolescents, housewives, and the elderly and chronic disabled who contribute to the bulk of mental disorder), we find that in England thirty-six million working days are lost each year from mental disorders. The rheumatic disorders are responsible for almost as many—thirty-five million days lost by the working population each year.

RHEUMATISM

The term "rheumatism" is a ragbag that includes a wide range of conditions. It was introduced in ancient times by Galen from the Greek word *rheo* (flow), at a time when medicine believed in the hour "humors" of the body whose flow was likely to be deranged; in rheumatism, through "acrimony of the humors," abnormal flow was thought to take place into various body vacuities—in gout, there were thought to be abnormal drops of humor (*guttae*) in the joints. It became the practice to refer to any sort of shifting pain as "rheumatism," although in the eighteenth century the term was applied mainly to the muscles. It was recognized that the joints could be involved, but secondarily to a muscular disorder.

In 1827, Scudamore, in a comprehensive treatise on rheumatism, stated he thought that the fleshy parts of muscle were not affected, but that the pain came from tendons and their fibrous insertions into bone. In 1904, Gowers wrote that muscular pain came from what he called "fibrositis"—a local inflammation of muscle,[13] although other workers in the field of study blamed either rigidity or weakness of muscle. At this time, Alexander began to explain his concept of mis-use, in which he proposed that attention should be paid to the *general* muscular co-ordination, and not simply to the local site of the pain in the muscle or joint. He also suggested—in majestic language— that the basic fault was psychophysical, and that it lay in "faulty pre-conceived ideas," "debauched kineasthesia," "inaccurate sensory appreciation."

Further research by leading rheumatologists led to the conclusion that "the muscles serve as a means of defence and attack in the struggle for existence: if the external expression of aggressiveness is inhibited, muscular tension may result which is felt as pain,"[14] and it was found that in 50 cases of muscular rheumatism 70% suffered from psychological disorders.

As electromyography came to be used, many people showed (Hench, 1946) that "psychogenic rheumatism is one of the commonest causes of generalised or localised aches and pains."[15] At the time, I stressed that we should not use the term "psychogenic": that it was not a question of the "psyche" doing something to the "soma," or the "soma" to the "psyche," rather that the rheumatism and the psychoneurosis are *both* of them manifestations of an underlying failure to achieve a balanced "resting state" of USE after stress.

Subsequently I published a study of students in which

the 10% who complained of persistent muscular pain all manifested a severely disturbed postural balance.[16] I suggested at that time that we should not talk about mis-use as being a psychosomatic disorder but rather that it should be considered as a "stress disorder": a stress disorder being one which habitually involves bodily systems beyond the relevant ones, and in which the organism does not return to a balanced resting state after activity. I suggested that bodily systems could be involved at four levels:

1. Physiological changes;
2. Emotional changes;
3. Behavioral changes; and
4. Structural changes;

and that all levels might be affected at the same time in the composite disorder of "mis-use." Rheumatism, in fact, as I saw it (and still see it), should never be considered simply in terms of the local part of the body that is malfunctioning, but should be taken in the context of mis-use of the whole body, involving as it does physiological changes, emotional changes, behavioral changes, and structural changes.

Part and parcel of this USE concept of rheumatism (and indeed of many other bodily disorders) is my disbelief in the "wisdom of the body." The body is not wise; it is usually stupid. For a human being to remain alive, certain variables must remain within definite limits. Many variables in our bodies—the length of our hair or the length of our nails—are not, except in a social sense, essential to life. The temperature and acidity of the blood, the amount of oxygen, sugar, salt, protein, fat, and calcium are of vital importance —a matter of life and death. They are kept constant by a ceaseless interplay of adjustments. Even if you don't drink for three days, the amount of water in your blood will change very little. If you then drink six quarts of water in six hours, the blood volume still won't change much, although the kidneys will have to work overtime to pour it out into the bladder. These mechanisms are on a stimulus-response basis. If there is too much swing away from the desired norm, the body, in its stimulus-response "wisdom," is stimulated to use one of its many systems to restore the balance. If its systems cannot come up trumps, it searches its environment for the necessary constituents—salt for the sweating miner, heroin for the junkie's transient "steady" state, alcohol for the liver that can no longer convert other food properly, nicotine for the quick energy of sugar release, sexual discharge for the irritable restless gonads, color and music to restore momentary peace to the restless brain.

This might seem like the wisdom of the body, but it is wisdom at a low level. It is the wisdom of end-gaining.

Consider another essential variable—your blood pressure. If by some mischance the part of your brain that usually regulates it is knocked out, another part of the brain will take over the job. If this part is knocked out, various ganglia outside the brain take over. If the ganglia are knocked out, the blood vessels themselves attempt, by contracting or enlarging, to regulate the pressure of the blood they contain.

The body, in fact, usually has several alternative ways of doing things. The body requires so much sugar in the blood, so much salt, so much oxygen and protein. It needs a familiar sense of muscular equilibrium as well as a state of calm. If these aren't met, the body begins to utilize—and, eventually, to damage—other systems or muscles. This is end-gaining, where the determination to get short-term ends on the basis of a reflex-stimulus response has a harmful effect on the body.

Reflex end-gaining does not pause to see whether the alternatives will be constructive or destructive in the long run. Such destructive alternativism is not wisdom. The badly burned body will recklessly pour out its body fluids through the burned surface until it dies from fluid loss. The asthmatic in his end-gaining anxiety to take in more and more air will use muscles in the upper chest in such a way that he cannot release them properly to let the used air out.

End-gaining, which uses potentially destructive procedures, is always a risky business, although much of our fortuitous evolution to date has been a result of it. We ourselves have it in us to decide our future in the spheres which we consider important. With all our shortcomings and conflicting systems and desires, we can still exercise our mind and act by deliberate intention. Instead of being at the mercy of a botched-up system of physicochemical reactions or muscular reflexes, we have it in us to become self-adjusting. We have it in us to live by principles that we have personally selected—a life of "constructive alternativism," using a new body-construct rather than a life of destructive alternativism.

USE AND RHEUMATISM

Nowhere is the "stupidity" of the body more apparent than in rheumatic disorders. Let us take as an example the condition of osteoarthritis of the hip joint. I am not concerned here with the factors that may have led to its development —although I suggest that mis-use is one of the most important—but with what happens when the condition is beginning to show itself. The earliest sign is a narrowing of the width of the joint, a narrowing that leads to shortening of the distance between the hip and the ground. This, in its turn, usually leads to further faulty distribution of body weight so that the weight is carried mainly through the affected hip. As a consequence of this wrongly distributed weight, the arthritic condition progresses and further shortening takes place on that side. This results in putting further weight on the affected hip joint, and so on, until the familiar picture of distortion and leg-shortening presents itself.

Such arthritis of the hip cannot be considered purely as a local event, although, of course, the time may come when local surgery is needed in dealing with the local condition. From a prevention or rehabilitation point of view, the use of the whole body has to be considered. When the early condition is starting to appear, attention must be given to the *general* use, to see that the balance is not thrown more and more onto the affected side.

This principle applies equally to such relatively slight but infuriatingly persistent conditions as "tennis elbow," painful stiff shoulders ("frozen shoulder"), and minor aches and pains in neck, chest, back, and legs. Certainly these conditions may disappear after rest or rubbing or injection or physiotherapy. But often they persist and become a source of worry and dissatisfaction with medical care. More often than not, these ailments will be associated with a small but undiagnosed disorder of the general USE. Plate 16 shows a young girl with just such a persistent leg pain whose tendency to stand with her weight incorrectly distributed was only noticed when she was accurately photographed against a grid.

The major use disorders of the spinal column are of far greater importance. The relevance of good use training in the various postural deformities of the spine—kyphosis, lordosis, and scoliosis—will be apparent. Even in spines that are severely affected, as in polio or idiopathic scoliosis, a great deal of help can usually be given to correct some of the deformity and to prevent its increase. By far the greatest number of patients seen in a rheumatology clinic (excluding the trivia, and arthritis affecting the limbs) will be one of two conditions: the cervical spondylosis and the almost pandemic pain in the back. These conditions are so prevalent and often so unresponsive to medical treatment

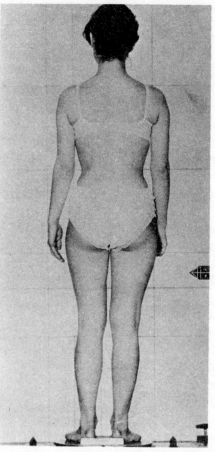

16. Patient standing on right leg. Central upright of grid should pass through middle of back and pelvis.

that they should each be considered here; in these two conditions the Alexander Principle has much to offer.

CERVICAL SPONDYLOSIS

Because the head-neck balance was thought by Alexander to be the primary seat of mis-use, he had much to say about symptoms which arise from that source. The varieties of mis-use in the head-neck region are infinitely complex. If we look again at the tiny sample of typically mis-used necks (Plates 2a, b, c, d, e), we see how much they vary, and yet an X-ray report on them never mentions even the presence of mis-use, much less the type of mis-use. Moreover, a still picture of a neck gives only slight indication of the nuances of muscular usage that are going on all the time, whether they be produced by speech, swallowing, gesturing, emoting, or searching the surroundings with the eyes or the ears.

The commonest of these mis-uses involves a drop forward of the middle of the neck, and this is accompanied by pulling the head back on the top of the neck. Plate 2d gives an example of this, although in time the neck has become so collapsed into the hump that it may not at once be obvious just how much collapse has taken place.

This collapse will involve tension of the muscles that go up into the back of the skull—not only the big external muscles (Fig. 22a, b, c) but also the smaller internal suboccipital muscles (Fig. 22d), which are placed around the junction of the neck and head. Much was—ill-advisedly—made of these small muscles by some of Alexander's earlier medical supporters, who encouraged him to believe in an almost magical potentiality in releasing these muscles to give full range to his "primary control."

Sometimes, instead of a collapsing of the neck forward, there will be an overstraightening of the neck, with a slight movement of the body and one of the neck vertebrae moving backward on the one below it. In my experience, these cases are usually associated with really intractable neck, head, or facial pain.

If we look at the neck from the back, we will often see a slight curvature sideways at the base of the neck, in the hump. This is usually ignored in X-ray reports, but again it

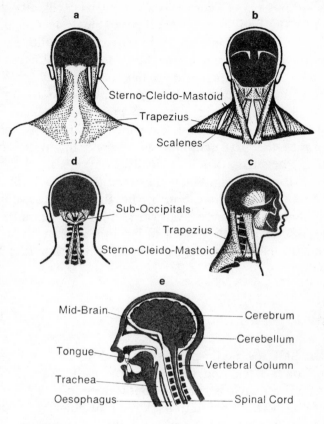

figure 22

is often associated with intractable symptoms. If you study the back of the neck, as in Plate 11a, you will notice two tense, contracted muscles just where they insert into the skull. When there is a sideways twist at the base of the neck, one of these two muscles will be more prominent than the other, and the resultant tension imbalance is even harder to release than the more symmetrical kind of faulty tension.

These and many more types of mis-use will always be found in the condition of cervical spondylosis (head and neck arthritis) or cervical disk pressure—conditions that affect 85% of us in our fifties. Most doctors will agree that they are difficult to treat and are long-lasting.

The usual symptom, at first, is numbness or tingling in the fingers of one hand, owing to pressure on nerve roots from the compressed and foreshortened neck vertebrae. Sometimes the first symptom is severe pain in the neck, shoulder, or arm, which typically is worse in the early hours of the morning, when the warmth of bedclothes has perhaps produced congestion in the already narrowed passages that carry nerves outward from the spinal cord. Sufferers find that they have to get up, or place their arm outside the bedclothes or in some new position to relieve the pain.

PAIN IN THE BACK

Over half the adult population of England experiences severe lower back and sciatic pain. Of the $450,000,000 estimated annual cost of rheumatic disorders, a high and increasing portion is due to back pain. Middle-aged workers with back trouble stay away from work for an average of five months, and since a large number of them are off work for less time than that, it means that a sizable proportion are away for more than a year.

In many cases, there may be some obvious immediate cause for the acute pain (a prolapsed disk or ankylosing spondylitis), but most of the people with painful backs will find themselves a diagnostic label such as "lumbosacral strain," "sacroiliac strain," "postural backache," "ligamentous strain," "fibrositis"—plus, from osteopaths, sophisticated labels like "facet block" or the unsophisticated label of an "osteopathic lesion."

Over a thousand possible reasons for back pain are cited in one American textbook. USE is not to be found among them. The failure to cope medically with back pain is exactly what might be expected where there is widespread ignorance of what constitutes a properly used back. Most forms of back pain, even after there has been unsuccessful surgery, are best treated by making USE re-education a prime necessity. Of course, there may be alleviation by manipulation, physiotherapy, injection, traction, corsets, and so on. However, the basic problem remains. These procedures do not alter the general manner of USE.

Only too frequently, disabling back pain attacks men and women of very high caliber who are making an important contribution in their chosen sphere. Often they will be under thirty years of age, and they face the prospect of crippling pain that will impose a restrictive pattern on their lives, whether it be in the rearing of their children or in the development of their working life. Eventually, after casting around for any conceivable therapy that might help, they resign themselves to a greatly limited existence, propped up by corsets and aspirins and loving relatives and friends. And very often they become profoundly depressed, since the mis-use pattern that led to their back trouble will, more often than not, contain a depressive-slump element in its components.

IT CANNOT BE EMPHASIZED TOO STRONGLY THAT IT IS WRONG TO TREAT A PAINFUL BACK AS A LOCAL CONDITION. BACK PAIN IS ALWAYS ACCOMPAINED AND PRECEDED BY GENERAL MIS-USE.

This general mis-use will have many variations. But usually three things are seen to be wrong. The thorax (chest cage) is thrown over to one side, and may be slightly rotated on the lumbar spine (Plate 17). The shoulder blades are raised, so that much of the muscular supporting work of the back is being done by the shoulders instead of the mid-back. And the breathing pattern is seen to involve a

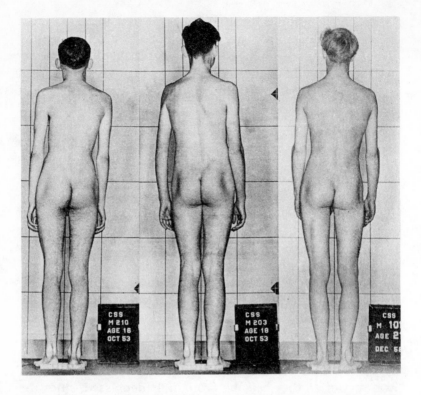

17. Three students with chests displaced to side. Note middle student, right shoulder back.

slight arching forward of the lumbar spine and the predominant habit of inhaling with the front of the chest and the abdomen. There will be many other associated tensions —depending on the type. An acute disk lesion will probably show flattening and rigidity; a chronic back may be hyperlordotic. A painful lower back must at first be dealt with by sorting out the mis-use of patterns in the neck and hump, since only when improved coordination can be maintained in the upper part of the back can there be improved use in the lower back and legs.

ARTHRITIS

Rheumatoid arthritis differs from osteoarthritis (a commonly found condition in various joints, resulting mainly from "wear and tear") in that it is a general systemic disease. It affects at least 1% of all males and 3% of all females. In mild cases there is little disability, but severe cases show advanced crippling and deterioration of the joints and tendons. It is another example of the "stupidity" of the body proving that its "adaptive" response is a major cause of the disease.

I doubt if anyone who has worked in this field would wish to deny the stress factor, but we are still faced with the question of why one person reacts with rheumatoid arthritis and another person doesn't. Indeed, the same question applies to most illnesses. Many of us can cite quite appalling psychological traumata or physical strains in our youth and maturity that we weathered in one way or another. Stress, in the event, depends on what seems like stress to any one of us—in other words, on our body-construct: the way we "construe" our situation, and the way we "structure" our response to it.

Rheumatoid patients exhibit a degree of muscular agitation that is not present in other rheumatic patients. I first noticed this in relation to excessive head movements made during speaking, but closer analysis shows a wriggling movement not only in the muscles of the spine but also in the limbs. Generally speaking, rheumatoid patients in the early stages of their condition tend to be "wrigglers," in a state of muscular agitation, and if they are not, it is either because the pathology has led to fixation or because pain and discomfort have induced them to keep still, or because they seek to control their agitation by excessive tension.

It is particularly in the communications situation that muscular agitation becomes apparent, and it may serve as an early diagnostic pointer.

Many of them are shy, sensitive people whose feelings are easily hurt—people with difficulty in communicating. This difficulty might account for the meticulous, orderly, conscientious life they like to lead, since they prefer an environment in which learned, stereotyped responses will suffice. It has struck me when dealing with them that because of this feeling of inadequacy in communicating, they resort to exaggerated muscular agitation. Many of them, by a sort of puppy-dog wriggling, put up a false front of niceness that belies their customary disposition. It seems to me within the bounds of possibility that this constant muscular restlessness may lead to joint dysfunction, and it cannot but be helpful to teach them a muscular resting state in which their exaggerated homeostatic swings are damped down.

PHYSICAL MEDICINE AND PHYSIOTHERAPY

Most hospital rheumatology departments combine their function with what is known as "physical medicine"—that is to say, the use of *physical* methods as opposed to *chemical* methods of treatment. This combining of functions has grown up from the fact that rheumatologists share with physical-medicine specialists the need for physiotherapists, trained in such physical methods. Today most physical-medicine specialists prefer to think of themselves as predominantly rheumatologists, mainly because of the link this gives them with general medicine, and also because the physiotherapist who carries on the actual day-to-day treatment on the patient comes to know a great deal more about the vagaries of muscle than the specialists do—although they might not admit it.

Much of physiotherapists' time—when it is not used in various methods involving electricity—is spent on the educating and re-educating of muscle. A major part of their work has to do with rheumatic disorders, but they are also involved in exercises of various kinds—prenatal and postnatal exercises, breathing exercises, mobilizing and strengthening exercises for the back, mobilizing fixed shoulders and knees and hips, correcting such postural defects as flat feet, knock-knees, winged shoulders, lordotic backs. Much time is given to the aftercare of people who have broken their bones, suffered amputation or nerve injury, or undergone serious orthopedic surgery to backs or hips or other regions. Both before and after an operation, patients in the wards are helped to become active sooner than they might be if they were left to their own devices. Time is devoted to rehabilitating patients who have had a stroke or suffer from long-lasting nervous diseases like multiple sclerosis or cerebral palsy. And, of course, a good part of the time is expended on "placebo" therapy, in which the friendliness of the physiotherapist and the comfort of massage, heat, and so on are major parts of the treatment. The varieties of procedures are immense but unfortunately they rarely include a knowledge of Alexander's approach.

Physiotherapists have been slower to learn Alexander's ideas than the modern physical education teachers. However, there is no doubt that before long the pressure of demand from patients will make it necessary for physiotherapy training schools to wake up to these ideas.

In all the types of situations mentioned above where physiotherapy is used—the rheumatic disorders, the spinal disorders, postural disorders, neurological disorders, breathing disorders, antenatal and postnatal care, general ward care and rehabilitation—the Alexander Principle is, in my opinion, of the greatest value. The only limiting factors are the availability of time and the capacity of the sick or elderly patient to cooperate. Restoration to the type of adequate functioning that is envisaged in this book is not achieved by our present hospital care, either in the wards or under outpatient care. To say this is not to decry the painstaking and devoted work that the physiotherapists and occupational therapists are performing, but to point out a gap in their training and their working procedures.

BREATHING DISORDERS

Nowhere is this gap more apparent than in the treatment of breathing disorders. To take one obvious example, the number of deaths from asthma is increasing, in spite of modern drugs that can counteract the acute attack. It is to no advantage simply to blame increased environmental stress, or more mites in the house dust! The explanation for the increase which tends to be overlooked is that *the asthmatic must be taught how to stop breathing the wrong way.* Breathing exercises have, of course, frequently been given by physiotherapists for this and other breathing conditions, but the fact is that breathing exercises as given at present will not help the asthmatic. Recent studies show that after such a course the majority of people breathe less sufficiently than when they started.

There is no shortage of information about the physiology of breathing; most of us know that too little oxygen or too much carbon dioxide will make us want more air, and we know that various reflex mechanisms in the brain, blood vessels, and lungs will work automatically to keep the breathing process going. This starts happening at birth, and stops when we die. However, a physiological account of reflex breathing does not tell us much about *how to breathe.* Unfortunately it is not only in the sphere of medicine that there is lack of knowledge in breathing technique. Actors, singers, speech teachers, and speech therapists have a special need to know about breathing, as, of course, have teachers of physical education. Yet in all these fields—medicine, communications, and physical education—there is a paucity of information about good breathing habits. The asthmatic does not need breathing exercises, he needs *breathing education.* He needs a minute analysis of his faulty breathing habits and clear instruction on how to replace them by an improved use of his chest. Moreover, chest USE cannot be separated from a consideration of the general manner of use. *All* patients with chronic bronchitis and asthma have a significantly high score in the Eysenck personality inventory, and the Cattell self-analysis form. Personality disorders increase as the chest trouble increases. To repeat it again, there is a very high correlation between personality scores and mis-use; i.e., increased neurosis goes hand in hand with increase in mis-use.

I have for several years given some very simple instructions to patients about their breathing, and these are reprinted in Chapter 8. As with all written instructions, however, five minutes of practical instruction is worth any amount of reading about it.

STRESS DISEASES

I have so far mentioned in this chapter many of the types of medical condition in which the Alexander Principle is most obviously needed. To this list should be added the diseases of civilization—the so-called stress diseases. While one would hope that knowledge of the Principle will lessen the incidence of these conditions, the role of the Principle for the most part will be in the lives of people who have already acquired a "stress" condition and who need to change their whole *modus vivendi.*

High on the list is hypertension—raising of the blood

pressure to the point at which there is a risk of cardiac damage or stroke. Emotional factors play a large part in raising the blood pressure. Frequently a patient's pressure will fall considerably when he is resting in the hospital or simply when he is less afraid of the medical situation in which he finds himself. I have known blood pressure to drop by as much as thirty points after a half-hour re-educational session in which tense muscles were relaxed. It seems crystal clear to me that since most blood vessels traverse or are surrounded by muscles, any overcontraction of the muscle is bound to squeeze the lumen of the blood vessels and thereby make it more difficult for the blood to be pumped through them by the heart. The less the obstruction to the blood flow, the less the pressure.

I see a good number of people who have had a coronary thrombosis. I have never yet seen a case in which the upper chest was not markedly raised and overcontracted.

Gastrointestinal conditions figure high in the list of stress conditions, whether it be gastric and duodenal disorders, spastic colon, ulcerative colitis, rectal spasm in the form of proctalgia, or anorexia nervosa in the young. Along with these, there are less easily defined symptoms of abdominal discomfort—compulsive air-swallowing, abdominal bloating and belching, frequent farting, and just simple constipation. And there is, of course, the undiagnosed pain in the stomach. The tenth most common cause of admission to the hospital in males—and the sixth most common in females —is unexplained abdominal pain which remains unexplained. In children and adolescents, it tends to be low down on the right side. In middle-aged people, it tends to be higher up, in the center. Children do not grow out of these pains; they have been shown to be still present twenty years later. Many patients have their appendix taken out, but that does not diminish the readmission rate to the hospital, which is high. It stands to reason that the fullest investigation must be carried out to see if there is pathological change, but where the investigation has been completed and treatment has not resolved the condition, it is often well to tackle the mis-use that invariably accompanied this condition. Patients with unexplained abdominal pain have a high Eysenck neuroticism score—and this, as we know, correlates closely with postural imbalance. More often than not, these patients are found to have a slight sideways displacement of the thorax on the lower back and often a rotary twist of the dorsolumbar spine, with associated muscle spasm. This should always be looked for in cases of unexplained abdominal discomfort.

A certain number of gynecological conditions—dysmenorrhea, retroversion of the uterus, and vaginismus—can be helped by this approach. Knowledge of how to maintain a stable integrated pattern of use is invaluable at the menopause—a time when the awareness of the postural model (the body-construct) may often become disturbed, with resultant feelings of unreality and depersonalization.

Perhaps the most obvious field for application is in the therapy of muscular tics and cramps, which can vary from the "occupational palsies," such as writers' and telephonists' cramps, to severe conditions like spasmodic torticollis and persistent spasm of the shoulders and trunk. I should mention here the condition of "atypical facial pain"—acute pain, usually across the nose, cheeks, and eyes, differing from trigeminal neuralgia in that it usually occurs in young adults. Anyone who has seen these patients—and the ineffectual way in which they have been treated—will not be surprised to learn that out of a group of six I saw (it is a relatively rare condition), four had made suicide attempts because of the pain, one of them after her jaw had been bound together by wire to immobilize the spasm. Re-education is arduous and takes many months, but all six cases became free from pain.

It is interesting that in his writings Alexander described torticollis and trigeminal neuralgia as two conditions that he had been able to help markedly. One must remember that in the past the Alexander Principle has often been a last-ditch effort, when everything else had been tried and the patients were severely distressed and disturbed by the chronicity of their condition—and, of course, skeptical of getting relief from yet another suggested therapy.

A final category that should be mentioned is accident-proneness, whether it be in cars or in the clumsiness of handling objects and one's general movements in everyday life. It has been found that a well-integrated person is less accident-prone. Indeed, it seems obvious that a better-balanced person is going to do himself less accidental damage and be less vulnerable to unexpected incidents or faults in his environment.

LOCAL VERSUS GENERAL

Clearly, such a conglomeration of bodily processes and uses must be integrated by a principle—a principle that permits of order and hierarchical structures, a hierarchy in which isolated parts of the body are not permitted to gain dominance over the well-being of the whole on an end-gaining basis. The Alexander Principle says that it is time to understand just how USE can be regulated to produce a stable equilibrium. It lays down procedures by which the conglomeration of potentially conflicting use patterns can be integrated into a hierarchical structure. It embodies this hierarchical structure in a newly learned body-construct, through which reflex "stupidity" comes under the influence of the "wisdom" of the brain. During Alexander's lifetime, it was believed he advocated a method of teaching people to control their functioning directly through their conscious mind. He never suggested—and it is not suggested here—

that we know enough about our physicochemical processes to attempt to control them by will, except perhaps on a research basis. (Rats can influence their heart rate, blood pressure, intestine movements, and urine formation; human beings likewise can be trained to reduce their blood pressure, by conditioning their autonomic control of blood vessels.) Such isolated control is at present more of a curiosity than a clinical tool. Rather, by establishing a principle of *chosen order* in the body's muscular USE, the autonomic system does not remain disordered after stress. A balanced resting state of use—in which individual parts do not gain dominance over other parts to which they should be subservient in the total hierarchy—appears to prevent the development of persisting autonomic imbalance.

The Alexander Principle applies right across the medical field. When someone gets ill, the sick part of his body is, of course, important. But what he does with the rest of his body in response to the sickness is equally important. The patient, as an example, feels ill because he has an acute sinus infection, but at the same time he will feel ill because he is using himself badly. The use patterns that he has developed over the years provide a context which predisposes him to his illness and also diminishes his resilience and capacity to adapt to the stress of the present illness. All this tends to be ignored by his doctor. The doctor thinks the patient is ill, because of his sinus, and the whole rigmarole of medical investigation is switched on to this. The sinus may indeed be making him feel ill, but a vast amount of the feeling of illness is based on bad USE. As soon as it is feasible, the patient's USE needs as much attention as does the specific pathology.

When and if the sinus trouble eventually clears up, the doctor will drop out of the picture, and from his point of view the patient is, for the time being, restored to normal health. The doctor will only have seen him on a few occasions, but the patient has to live with himself always, and he has to live with his persisting habits of wrong USE. His doctor finds "no demonstrable disease"; no descriptive disease label may now be pinned on him. But in spite of this, wrong habits of USE persist and lead the patient to feel continuously fatigued and unwell, to the point when the strain of making any extra effort outside his everyday life may far outweigh personal gain or social pleasure.

Investigations that were carried out at the Peckham Health Centre showed that out of 1,666 normal individuals who were examined, there were 1,505 cases of classifiable disease, but in addition to this the investigators found a widespread condition of devitalization, characterized by an overwhelming sense of fatigue and loss of vitality.

Nowadays it is popular to have general "health screening" of men and women over the age of fifty to exclude serious illness, but, alas, as yet such health screening does not include an analysis of their mis-use. An investigation into problems of disease and devitalization must take into account the persistent influence of USE in every reaction and during every moment of life. A diagnosis that ignores this influence is incomplete. Any plan of treatment that fails to take it into account must leave behind a predisposition to disease and malfunctioning.

RECOMMENDED STEPS

So I make the following suggestions for the use of the Alexander Principle in medicine:

1. Preventively: during the school years (at least), the doctors, physical education instructors, dance teachers, and schoolteachers should be aware of mis-use in the children under their care. Some indication should be made on the child's record and any deterioration noted.

2. Therapeutically: the USE factor should be included in the various systems that are examined by doctors, not merely (as at present) as a cursory analysis of joint mobility, integrity of the reflexes, muscular power, and so on, but as a bodily system in its own right, as important as any other bodily system. No medical student should complete his training without being given some knowledge of the USE factor.

3. In hospital medicine, there must be a new concept of rest, so that the patient who is lying in bed supposedly resting is not setting up excessive dystonic patterns.

4. Specifically, it must be used in the care of rheumatic, orthopedic, neurological, psychosomatic, and mental disorders.

5. In order to do this, nurses and physiotherapists should be instructed about USE. Not only will it help them in handling their patients, but it will give them personally an additional way of coping with the stresses and strains of hospital life. And heaven knows there is plenty of stress for nurses in a world in which trivial matters are apt to gain too much importance—a world often full of rigid rules and hierarchy, a world in which the personality has to be constantly adapted to suit different patients, and yet a world in which there is lack of scope for initiative.

6. In industry, the present work of ergonomic research should be extended. Scientists and factory doctors must learn to detect situations which encourage mis-use, and to observe correctable mis-use in workers.

The preventive implications of the Alexander Principle must be promoted everywhere by those interested in health education. The resources of television, radio, and published articles must be used to make these facts more widely known.

People must be trained specifically in teaching the Principle, in order to help those who fall into the above categories. The size of the problem should not deter the much needed wide-scale attack.

CHAPTER 5

Mental Health

It has been suggested that if a concept could be found in the field of mental health that was as basic as MASS is in physics, then the whole subject would be revolutionized. USE may well be just that basic concept.

It is not ideas that are responsible for neurosis. It is the way we react to our ideas with dystonic use patterns that constitutes the neurosis. This cannot be emphasized too strongly. The reason it has not seemed obvious in the past is that prior to Alexander's work, there had never been an adequate microanalysis of dystonic use patterns. Until his concept of USE was established, no criterion could be adopted that would tell us in what ways a mentally sick person was departing from good use.

Much behavior that passes for normal already contains traces of neurotic mis-use. Such pre-neurotic mis-use patterns are usually ignored or not recognized until they have developed to the point of seeming definitely odd. Before the development of the odd behavior, the mis-used person may have been thought simply to have the "normal abnormalities" that go to make up most people's personality. Only after improved use patterns have been developed does it become clear just how much the previous mental disorder was based on an inadequate manner of use; such a manner of use will be seen to return if the neurotic pattern returns.

Anxiety and Muscle Tension

I spent the greater part of ten years working very closely with Alexander, often just with him, myself, and one patient in the room, and it soon appeared to me that his work could provide a way of detecting and observing mental states that no other process could provide in such tangible form. Behind his theories of the "primary control," and a seemingly gymnastic preoccupation with getting people to sit down and stand up without upsetting the tension balance of their necks and heads, lay a constant preoccupation with the "chosen" and "unchosen" components of behavior.

One of the earliest medical articles that I wrote on his work, in 1947, was entitled "Anxiety and Muscle Tension," and it was obvious to me then that his approach was very relevant to the handling of neurotic disorders.

The connection between anxiety states and muscle tension is now generally accepted, and drug firms have been quick to fill the doctor's letter box with expensive circulars that purport to show just how anxiety can be relieved by their tension-relaxing drugs. But in 1947 the general psychiatric opinion was that "in anxiety states there is no known structural or chemical variation which accompanies the all too obvious symptoms" Gregg, 1944), and that "if we consider the long list of psychoneurotics with their hysterias, anxieties, obsessions and states of inexplicable fatigue and depression, there is no characteristic physical accompaniment which can be detected by present methods."[17] At that time, I knew from Alexander's work that there was indeed a very definite physical accompaniment—i.e., muscular over-activity and mis-use—to psychoneurosis.

In the succeeding years it became clearer, by the use of electrical methods of recording muscle tension, just how close the correlation could be between mental states and muscular states. For example, arm tension was found to be connected with hostility; buttock and thigh tension with sexual problems. In many other ways, it became apparent that the mentally sick were physically tense. One of the most striking observations at that time was made by Wolff, who found over 90% of headache sufferers produced their pain, albeit unwittingly, by "marked sustained contraction in the muscles of the neck," and that such muscular contraction was associated with "emotional strain, dissatisfaction, apprehension and anxiety."[18]

Over the past twenty years, many people have followed up these observations on mind and muscle. A recording which I made years ago illustrates the point (Fig. 23). It compares the electrical activity in a person's forearm when an actual movement of the hand is being made with the activity that occurs when the hand movement is only being *thought* of. This is an astonishing indication of the link-up of mind and muscle, and various people of the behaviorist school have

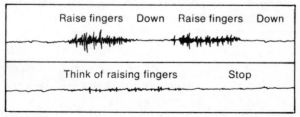

figure 23

suggested that it is impossible even to *think* of an activity without causing small contractions in the muscles which, enlarged, would produce the actual movement. Indeed, it has been claimed by some people that thinking itself is always accompanied by such small muscular movements. The early behaviorists considered small movements of the vocal muscles or of the muscles of the eyes likely vehicles of thought. It is tempting to follow up such ideas, but it seems to me more likely that the undoubted overactivity which occurs in certain muscles when we are engaged in thinking is in fact an unnecessary mis-use, and simply gives further indication of how easily most of us will produce unresolved dystonic patterns in response to quite minor ideas.

Tension During Communication
Tension patterns which arise during movement are quite different from those which are triggered off by the procedure of communication. The processes of searching and selecting to connect up and communicate with other people are deeply embedded in our character structure and may not be at once apparent as obvious mis-use patterns. Communication does, of course, take place in a most obvious way by word and gesture; bodily "mood signs" are the stock in trade of any actor, and easy to observe. But, in addition to these *obvious* gestures and postures, we find in most people tiny use patterns that unconsciously, automatically—and whether people like it or not—transmit a certain mood, often quite contrary to their intention in expressing themselves.

Recent writings on "body language" and "body awareness" have stressed the importance of such nonverbal communication. But many of these forms of USE can be observed only under conditions of minute analysis, which Alexander was the first to employ. One of Alexander's greatest contributions lay in his method of observing tiny dystonic patterns. He realized that most of these patterns would show up *when a patient was asked to learn something new.* Above all, he observed them without tiresome instrumentation, and within the context of an acceptable everyday learning situation.

Some of us may be aware of a slight clenching of our hands when we are angry or of hunching our shoulders and fixing our chest when we are afraid, or fidgeting movements when we are anxious. But many other tension states occur below the level of our consciousness, although they contribute a great deal to the general background of our personal awareness. Such tension states form patterns that may be among the most delicate and sensitive means of communication we have at our disposal, even though they easily become irrelevant, unchosen, unconscious habits.

Often these tensions include fragments of some role that was significant in the past but is now irrelevant. They may appear suddenly at quite inappropriate moments, and they may evoke from those around us reactions we do not want. Unless there is knowledge of a basic balanced resting state of USE, such tensions are likely to build up into attitudes that undermine our interpersonal relationships without our knowing it.

In many cases, the emotional tension may be quite obvious and land us in trouble then and there—for example, in the sudden muscular cramps that affect writers, carpenters, typists, musicians, cow-milkers, dentists, golfers (at the top of the back swing), billiard players (unable to bring the cue forward), and many others. A recent patient of mine, when he lifted a glass or a teacup, would get stuck with his cup halfway to his mouth.

These tension states often occur in a setting where there is emotional strain. Writer's cramp has been attributed to anger that is unexpressed or denied—anger that leads first to a clenching of the forearm and hand and then to the adoption of increasingly bizarre shoulder and neck postures in an attempt to counteract the arm-clenching. In the same way, unwanted sexual feeling may be counteracted by making excessive leg and pelvic tensions.

In most of these dystonic patterns, it is not easy to separate a physical reason from a psychological reason. The way we construe our surroundings—the way we seek to *construct* our surroundings to our taste—is a psychophysical act in which mind cannot be separated from muscle for long.

MIND AND MUSCLE

In spite of his old-fashioned stimulus-response approach, Alexander was insistent on psychophysical relatedness. The relation of mind to muscle has often been seen as a *mens sana in corpore sano* approach (and its corollary *mens insana in corpore insano*). This sort of uncomplicated cheeriness appeared in a popular book by J. E. Goldthwaite, entitled *Body Mechanics* (1952). "When the body is used rightly, all of the structures are in such adjustment that there is no particular strain in any part. The physical processes are at their best, the mental functions are performed most easily, and the personality or spirit of the individual possesses its greatest strength." There are reminders here of William James (1915): "Thus the sovereign voluntary path to cheerfulness, if our spontaneous cheerfulness is lost, is to sit up cheerfully, to look around cheerfully, to act and speak as if cheerfulness were already there."

How is such a "sitting up" obtained? There are myriad ways of straightening and myriad ways of slumping the various parts of the body. The slumped posture is not the only opposite of sitting up straight. The body is not simply a system of mechanical levers, to be adjusted into different positions like a mechanical crane. It is a subtle organ of expression, in which emotional states modify and are modified by muscular tension states. Indeed, William James knew all about this when he wrote: "By the sensations that so incessantly pour from the over-tense excited body, the over-tense excited habit of mind is kept up: and the sultry threatening exhausting thunderous inner atmosphere never quite clears away." His sovereign remedy of "sitting up cheerfully" is unlikely to get rid of the "thunderous inner feelings" as long as unresolved dystonic patterns persist.

Nevertheless one should not forget the role of courage in the mind-muscle relationship. Courage is clearly present in four-minute milers, in mountaineers, in riders from Ghent to Aix, and even in the everyday man who exerts will power to take the plunge into a cold bath or the sea. We are familiar with the stories of paralyzed and amputated veterans learning to walk, painfully, step by muscular step. These cases, admirable and truly heroic, can be seen daily in rehabilitation departments throughout the country.

In the everyday world, the "courageous" use of muscle has tended recently to fall into disrepute except as part of the weekend gladiatorial scene on the football field or in the athletic arena. A recoil to the shuffling discotheque has followed; but there has also followed an interest in the less violent use of muscle—a use that will permit and not preclude clarity of thought and emotion. It is with the less violent use of muscle that we are concerned here.

ATTITUDE AND EMOTION

In his book *The Expression of the Emotions* (1872), Darwin used the term "expressive action" to denote movements, gestures, and attitudes from which the existence of an underlying state can be inferred, and he considered that "such movements of expression reveal the thoughts of others more truly than do words which may be falsified." More recently, phrases like "nonverbal communication" and "body language" have appeared, and it has become a commonplace that emotional attitudes of, say, fear and aggression are mirrored immediately in muscle; such moods as happiness, excitement, and evasion are thought to have their characteristic muscular patterns and postures. The depression in Plate 18a is obvious, as is the gradual improvement shown in Plates 19b and 19c.

There is nothing very new in this thought. Saint Augustine wrote in the fifth century, *"Hoc autem eos velle ex motu*

18. Collapse and depression. Loss of depression with loss of collapse.

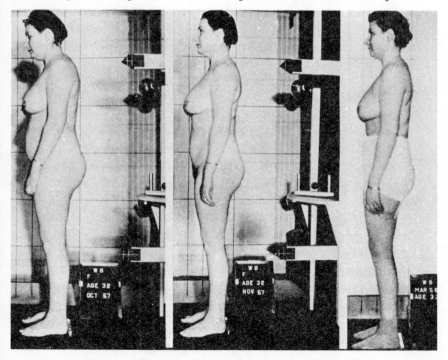

corporis aperiebatur: tanquam verbis naturalibus omnium gentium" ("Their intention became apparent through their bodily movement, as it were the natural language of all people") (*Confessions* 1).

It is not unusual that most of us adopt the attitude of those we are with, and especially of those we love; even in the cinema, we may mimic those we identify with—which may account for vigorous feelings that come on, for example, after a James Bond picture. A family posture is often the expression of a basic family mood. Rejection of the family mood may lead to rejection of the family posture: "I can't stand like that, it feels just like the way my mother looks," one girl with a chronic back pain said to me after her posture had been temporarily corrected. She preferred her pain to her parent's posture.

And indeed changing such ingrained postures usually does cause repercussions in interpersonal relationships. I was consulted by a civil servant who had severe shoulder pain as a result of an ingrained attitude of cringing. It was possible to get him to release the tension by which he was deforming himself, and in his new state he was free from pain. However, his attitude of cringing before superiors was so ingrained that he would sooner lose what he had been taught, and give himself pain, than not appear "humble." Not until he eventually had a flaming row with his boss and stood up for himself was he able to maintain his improved pain-free attitude.

Deforming attitudes of cringing and evasiveness eventually lead to structural change. The evasive action of turning the gaze away by rotating the head will eventually set up a permanent twist in the neck.

The "attitude theory of the emotions" is fine as far as it goes, but it is still at a crude behavioral level. The cases I cited above—which could be multiplied almost indefinitely —do indeed say that the body has its language and that we have for too long neglected the important messages which are sent out in that language. But the crude James-Lange approach, which says that the attitude *is* the emotion, does not do justice to the facts. Almost any emotion can get latched on to almost any habitual muscle-tension trick. The named emotions—anger, fear, jealousy, evasion, cowardice, courage, and so on—are only a fraction of the multitudinous shades of emotional feeling that go on in all of us. Most of these feelings have no particular names. They are part of the background of our general awareness—a background that is sustained by our particular USE.

Even at this crude macroscopic level of observable "body language," the message may not be an immediate one. *Many habitual postures do not represent an immediate expression of an emotion*, but are rather *a position from which certain actions and emotions can be possible.* The slumped collapsed adolescent is confused at first if he adopts an improved USE, because most of his favored interpersonal reactions become impossible with this new use. It is only from his old slumped and twisted state that he feels able to communicate with those he likes. The old posture is the position from which he can express certain emotions and from which he cannot express others. His particular posture is not necessarily connected with any particular emotion, although eventually a state of depression will be only too easily induced by his state of slump.

Indeed, many of these postures do not start as emotional response, but rather from the way we use our bodies in recurrent work situations. The office workers, the conveyor-belt engineer, the dentist, the pianist—all carry out certain occupations for so long that they eventually hold themselves partially contracted even when they are not involved in the actual pressures and resistances of their jobs. Though this residual tension may not be conscious, it is finally maintained most of the time. The result of the various temporary attitudes finds its expression in a posture—or in a limited repertoire of postures—which eventually dominates a person's character. Deforming postures are the result of the gain in strength in certain specific muscles that have never been properly released, until it becomes easier to rest and to move within the familiar deformed structures. In small and at first unobtrusive ways, we become enslaved to our past.

THE RESTRUCTURING OF USE

Alexander saw, as many have seen, that what was needed was a better way to help a person reconstruct his life so that he need not be a victim of his past. But he attempted such a restructuring at the fundamental level of USE, on a general rather than a specific basis, and in a way not attempted by other forms of psychological treatment. No one could claim that drugs or shock treatment restructure a person's USE, except in the crudest sense. The alternatives of individual or group psychotherapy, in which a person's ideas and constructs are examined and worked through, is of course an advance on crude physical treatments; but the inescapable fact remains that all neurotic people mis-use themselves. I have never yet seen a neurotic person who did not show dystonic patterns. Accordingly, the Alexander Principle asserts that, in the therapy of neurotic disorders, any form of drug treatment or psychotherapy which ignores the USE factor is inadequate.

The Alexander approach reverses the psychotherapeutic approach. The psychotherapist says, "You will only get rid of your unwanted behavior in a satisfactory way when your mental attitudes have been sorted out." The Alexander Principle says, "It will be impossible to sort out your mental attitudes in a satisfactory way as long as you persist with that faulty manner of use." Not that I do not applaud the insights of psychotherapy and psychoanalysis; but if we recognize mis-use as a comprehensive attempt to deal with our personal experience of emotional distress, there is no need to give priority to discovering a psychological cause for that mis-use. Rather, the priority should be discovering an improved manner of use. From this vantage point, the now controllable mis-use patterns can be detected, and resolved when they arise.

Psychotherapy seeks to give us insight into why we have taken up specific attitudes. This, however, can be only one of the aspects of the formation of tension habits. It may well be that a given muscle-tension habit started at some specific time, possibly as the result of a severe trauma, or as a casual unimportant accidental trick that was discovered and seemed to fit a given circumstance at a time when the general use pattern was already becoming disturbed. At whatever time and however these tension habits were learned, an adult will have perfected them (and many other tricks) until they are thereafter integrated with his behavior.

The inertia, the necessity, the comfort—however slight—of the established way of life will continue to provoke tension habits and to keep them in existence. They will stay in existence until a thorough re-education of mis-use patterns has taken place. With the best will and the best insight from the best psychiatrists in the world, we can eventually only tackle our tension habits by unlearning them at each actual moment of behavioral reaction, and this means the establishment of a *consciously structured pattern of use*. The Alexander way of establishing a newly structured USE is described in Part 2. Let us consider here how USE can be seen as a cause of mental disorder.

First we need to understand what a "cause" is. There are all sorts of causes.

If you throw a stone at a brittle glass window, it will break, and under similar circumstances it would always break. But there are more causes than the stone. If I hadn't *wished* to throw the stone, the window would still be intact. If it had been a Ping-Pong ball, the window would still be intact. If the window had been as tough as a car windshield, it might not have shattered. Three sorts of causes: my wanting it; the stone; the brittleness of the window.

These are usually called:

1. Final-cause motivation: i.e., my wish for a certain end, or for the consequences that flow from that end—e.g., so that I can lift a diamond bracelet from the window display.

2. The efficient (or effector) cause: i.e., the actual moving factor that does it—in this case, the stone.

3. The dispositional cause: i.e., the circumstances that make it possible—the brittleness of the glass, the absence of police. This disposition of the glass is a latent capacity that exhibits itself when the circumstances arise.

Let me take another example. I am frying an egg in a frying pan, over a gas flame. The final cause (my motivation) is that I want the end (i.e., a fried egg).

The efficient (effector) cause is the gas flame: I turned on the gas—the first step—lit it, and now it burns. I would not have turned it on without some sort of decision to do so—the decision born of my final cause.

And finally there is the dispositional cause. An egg is disposed to coagulate when heated, because of its chemical composition.

WHICH CAUSE?

Which of these three types of cause are we to blame for a mental disorder? Which of them can we alter?

When people put forward several explanations of something, the explanations are not really *rival* explanations—they are answers to different questions. There are as many sorts of explanations as there are questions—it is simply a matter of priorities. The causes (antecedents) that matter are the ones that can be altered; and usually the chief causes tend to be the ones that a particular speaker thinks *should* be altered.

Disputes among psychiatrists about causes could more realistically be stated as disputes about treatments. The true cause lies deep in the psyche (psychotherapy needed); the true cause lies in the brain chemistry (drugs needed); the true cause lies in conditioned reflexes (behavior therapy needed).

These three rivals may not be clear-cut and may overlap in their methods at times, but, by and large, they remain distinct. Three different causes are postulated. Three different approaches are recommended.

These three different schools of psychiatric thought range themselves around the three "causes" that I have mentioned —"dispositional causes," "final causes," and "efficient causes." The dispositionists search for a chemical or physical predisposition in the brain that may lead to abnormal behavior. At present they have only crude chemical notions of what this might be; they use elementary blunderbuss chemicals with which to alter the brain chemistry, and do not mind if they alter other chemistry, which is not faulty, at the same time. Alternatively they may use crude physical methods such as Electroconvulsive Therapy or leucotomy to alter ingrained brain dispositions.

The final-causists (the various schools of psychotherapy) work to find the decision that was once taken to "throw the stone or fry the egg," a decision that perhaps was once consciously chosen and deemed appropriate, but has now become unchosen and inappropriate. If we try to sort out neurotic mis-use in terms of such final-cause motivation, we can perhaps find out eventually (over months, years, or even decades) what the patient's "game" was that started a particular tension manifestation. The tension trick by now is so much a part of him that it will be released simply by his discovering its cause. The patient may come to terms with it, but much of it remains embodied in his whole life pattern, and in the muscular usages through which it is expressed.

The third cause—the efficient cause—has as its champions the schools of behavior therapists, who attempt to alter the conditioned reflexes that have become embedded in the life pattern, whatever the original reason for the conditioning. But they are at a disadvantage—an unnecessary disadvantage. They do not know enough about mis-use, and they work with an ethology of macro-behavior—relatively gross observable behavior—and not at the all-important microanalysis of USE.

Aversion therapy and deconditioning used by behaviorists to tackle writers' cramps and phobias are crude stuff indeed. Their operant conditioning techniques often appear terrifyingly aggressive to anyone used to the subtlety of the Alexander concept of muscular use.

The Alexander Principle takes all three causes of mental ill health into account: the final cause—the choice—by the remaking of the body image, and by teaching the new faculty of "ordering"; the efficient cause—the muscular reaction—by thorough muscular analysis, undreamed of by the behaviorists; and the dispositional cause—the resting state —by a gradual re-education of the postural attitude and disposition, rather than by an instantaneous chemical or physical onslaught. The resting state is manifested in the patient's *general use pattern*. Through the changes produced in the postural attitude, a new disposition, based on a new core structure, can slowly be constructed.

With all three causes included in the practical learning situation, the Alexander procedure makes the following points:

1. No psychological diagnosis is complete unless USE is carefully considered.

2. Help and insight may be gained through psychotherapy, but will not themselves alter the habits of USE. Unchanged habits of USE will provide a soil in which further mental disorder can grow.

3. Insights perceived in a very disturbed state of USE are not necessarily to be trusted.

4. Accordingly, it should be a priority in mental treatment to obtain the best possible resting state of balanced USE before embarking on treatment. The same applies to group therapy.

5. The success of any given treatment (whether by psychotherapy, behavior therapy, drugs, or shock treatment) should be assessed by its effect on the general USE and not just by its success in putting the patient back into circulation. There is as much USE insanity in the streets as in the wards of our hospitals.

CONCLUSION

It should now be clear that the Alexander Principle is neither predominantly psychological nor predominantly physical but *psychophysical*, somewhere between the analysts and the behavior therapists, between the prayers and the drugs, between psyche and soma.

If you will acquire a more balanced USE, you will be able to go into new surroundings and accept new experiences (or old experiences that have previously troubled you) without the old degree of strain. Not right away but gradually, you will find new ways of connecting up with things and people, without fear or stress.

CHAPTER 6

The Psycho-Mechanics of Sex

Sex, when it is right, is the pleasantest, most desirable, most enjoyable activity. It takes a lifetime of study and sensitivity to explore its possibilities. It goes devastatingly wrong for all of us at times; it goes miraculously right for most of us, often when we least expect or deserve it. Like everything else, it is facilitated and hindered by the sensitivity of our manner of use. It is exacting and it is mysterious. We can never quite know what will switch the current off or on.

There is no firm agreement about what is right and good in sexual matters. Variegated guilt-free sex with many partners—aided, if necessary, by drugs that are believed to be relatively harmless—is set against long-lasting "normal" sex, in which the same male organ is, more often than not, in apposition with the same female organ. On the one hand, magic is sought from technical variety and drugs; on the other, from an experience that can grow and develop over a lifetime of "normal" intercourse with one partner. Both sides see the other side as wrong: "promiscuous" on the one hand, "old-fashioned" on the other. Both seem to desire a "good" that is incompatible with the "good" the other wants.

In a scientific society, no doubt some sociologist-*cum*-anthropologist-*cum*-psychologist could eventually produce evidence to show that matched controls (just imagine trying to get sufficient numbers, let alone following them up for at least twenty years!) were happier following a variegated sex life than the old-fashioned "normal," or vice-versa. In the absence of such unobtainable scientific evidence, all that can be suggested are certain immediate biological principles, which will hold good for sexual behavior whatever the culture.

Such is the power of our early training that most of us are cautious about where our sexual feelings may take us. The young adolescent girl who had been told by her mother that she must never let a man touch her, and thereafter sat rigid in buses in case a man should accidentally come into contact with her, seems ridiculous to us. Yet the initial explosion of sex at adolescence makes most people wary of their sexual reflexes, and they may soon learn to stifle even the slightest stirrings.

The psychoanalysts have not helped in this matter. Until recently it has been thought undesirable for an analyst to have any physical contact with the patient who is being analyzed, and my own re-educational work, which involves almost continuous handling and adjustment and training of the body, has seemed to some analysts to be inviting disastrous transference situations. Yet this does not take place in any harmful sense. Not only is it necessary for patients to be handled in order to learn how to use themselves properly, it is also positively beneficial for them to realize that in this situation they can be touched and adjusted without fear and danger—that they are not going to be raped or feel the need to make instant onslaught on whoever happens to be around.

In *Eros Denied,* Wayland Young has pointed out how it is that around the thought and act of sex there hang "a confusion and a danger, a tension and a fear which far exceed those hanging over any other normal and useful part of life in our culture." In the 1970s, the sexual revolution that Wilhelm Reich preached has tried hard to get under way, but the revolution has been primarily concerned with the *physical* mechanics of sex: sex supermarkets, school instruction, the pill, easier abortion, less reluctance to make love, less social censure, better facilities for sexual voyeurism. It is one thing to have the means and mechanics for sex, it is quite another to practice an art that can encompass the ugliness of the jerking dog and the beauty of Marcus Perennius. Plastic-doll beauty, on stage and screen, with simulated coition, tells us little or nothing about the all-important psycho-mechanics of sex, which are as invisible as our breathing, as subtle as the tiny brushstrokes of a Chinese calligrapher.

SEXUAL MANNERS OF USE

Sexual activity involves the sharpening of all the senses. In it, the human faculties of searching, selecting, and interconnecting are employed with an intensity that is scarcely matched in any other sphere of life.

The key word is responsiveness: the responsiveness of our own body to touch and movement, the sensed response of the partner, but mainly our responsiveness to our own feelings.

Muscular responsiveness is a matter of "feedback," by which our perception of sensation is adjusted and controlled by a "body-construct" in which we "construe" what is happening and then "construct" the preferable muscular reaction.

Feedback can be of two kinds: *negative* feedback, in which, like a thermostat, mechanisms of balanced sensitivity adjust the temperature so that it doesn't get out of hand; or *positive* feedback, in which each fresh stimulus adds to the intensity of the muscular reaction that is providing the stimulus, so that it provokes yet more of the stimulus —similar to positive feedback of an atomic explosion in which a chain reaction of stimulus and response becomes uncontrollable in a matter of milliseconds.

Sexual responsiveness, quite obviously, involves both negative and positive feedback. By negative feedback, sexual stirrings are not allowed to go over too soon into an uncontrollable positive feedback situation. But such is the cultural fear of positive feedback that even the slightest stirrings of sexual pleasure may be stifled, and the opposite poles of sexual deadness and sexual explosion may come to constitute an "either-or" situation, which leaves a vast intermediary territory unsensed and unexplored.

EROTISM

Our language has a shortage of words that refer to this vast intermediary territory and there are few words to describe experiencing the erotic pleasure that does not lead to immediate orgasmic discharge. To feel "sexy" or "randy" implies a state of lust that already sounds either naughty or reprehensible. Far be it from me to decry the whole language and lore of the dirty story, which we learn from our earliest school days and which remain, graffiti scribbled on the walls of our cerebral cortex, long after more important and beautiful ideas have disappeared. But there are also erotic words that we do not seem to possess, words for experiences that do not nightly devour us with passion and that we have no particular need to resist. To talk, for example, of "eroticism" brings in a boudoir tinge of sensuality far from the everyday pleasure in our muscles and skin which should be part of our moment-to-moment bodily awareness. "Erotism" seems to me perhaps a better word, if it can be freed from the overtones of guilt that the Freudian phrase "autoerotism" gave it. Words may not seem all that important, but words are signposts, and we sorely need words for this realm of awareness and bodily pleasure which may have no immediate sexual implication, although it is part of the sexual spectrum.

MUSCULAR TEXTURE

Erotism is concerned as much with the *texture* of bodily experience as with its *structure*. When texture is lost, the body feels blunted or deadened. Action may occur (action to gain ends), but the satisfaction lies more in the achievement than in the actual doing. The accent is on specific objects, isolated from their background, instead of on the texture of the background.

The Gestalt psychologists, although out of fashion nowadays, encouraged us to think of perception in terms of "figure" and "ground."[19] To take a simple example, a countryman who comes up to London finds the traffic noise deafening, the filthy streets disgusting. The noise and the dirt stand out as "figures" against the groundwork of his expectations. But a Londoner has long since lost the traffic noise in a general background—he does not notice it. Instead he notices the number of an approaching bus or other "figures" important to him. A police-car siren or perhaps a jet plane may stand out momentarily as a "figure," but even these may soon become background for more immediate figures.

In the control of sexual perception, we are dealing very much with such a "figure-ground" situation; by thought and by movement we can turn our attention from one part to another, from one "figure" to another, until with muscular sensitivity and feedback we gradually build up a generally heightened awareness of bodily texture. The concern should not simply be with structure, but with the development and recognition of texture.

Texture—as the computors have proved, whether it be in the microanalysis of a painting or of a fabric—is based on *order;* and it is based on the repetition of order, in a certain progression along certain hierarchies. If hierarchical order is lost, texture is lost.

Texture, in the context of sexual perception, is built up of a repetitive order that gives an ongoing progression from one state to the next. In sexual perception, as in everyday living, the textural quality of our muscular experience is obtained by a correct order of the structural USE of our body, and by a refusal to fix the ongoing progression of movement by muscular tension. Texture is destroyed by tension.

Such tension may be a deliberate defense, or it may be unconscious. When sexual feeling begins to invade the texture of our muscular experience, it may not always be welcome. Negative feedback is usually adequate to regulate and enjoy the everyday felicities of erotism (although even these may be blocked by overtension): during a period of transition, in which an ongoing sexual progression induces positive feedback and begins to take over, muscle-tension brakes are liable to be clamped right down.

Characteristic of the beginnings of such ongoing sexual feelings are sensations that can be described as "floating" or "falling," or "lightness" or even gluey "heaviness." Many of us are afraid of such sensations. The sensation of being anesthetized gives such a sense of progressive falling into ourselves, and most of us will have experienced certain situations in which, momentarily, all visible means of support disappear and we feel ourselves falling.

It needs a certain courage not to attempt to counteract such feelings of falling or floating. To "let go" into someone's arms may be infinitely reassuring, but it does not mean that once the weight is off the feet, it will be possible to let go all the habitual dystonic patterns of our lifetime. Even the most erudite employer of the most erudite sexual skills and approaches will find that both he and his partner are thrown out of gear and out of pleasure by dystonic patterns. Appearing for no apparent reason, these patterns may effectively kill off feeling and desire and the natural progression toward orgasm, or may modify the quality and the timing of feelings so that both are unsatisfactory.

There are some people for whom love-making is never very satisfactory and in whom the onward "textural" progression of muscular release is constantly replaced by feelings of tension. Instead of erotic feelings of floating and lightness, they experience feelings of trying hard and of effort—indeed sometimes cramp and pain—or there may be a deadening and blunting of sensation.

When texture is replaced by tension, sexual responsiveness may come to be equated with relatively violent movement. Many women feel that they must exhibit by the intensity of their body movements and the wildness of their breathing and voice that they are in no way frigid. They may even persuade themselves in so doing that this is what it is all about.

Sexual responsiveness is not a matter of wild movement except insofar as positive feedback releases the reflexes. It is a matter of the handling of subtle differential feelings of expansion and swelling, of systole and diastole, throughout the whole body. It is about the balancing of muscular reactions, and it is about the correct "ordering" of muscular reactions, to produce texture.

THE ORDER OF REACTION

Like the orchestra conductor who allowed the demands of his baton to override the needs of the rest of his body, many people by overconcentration on specifically genital movements and sensations begin to induce in themselves a general fixation and rigidity, which in its turn restricts natural progression through the many phases of love-making. (In passing, it is nice to remember that, according to the fourteenth-century Cabalists, the total number of angels is 301,655,722. This number is not surprising when we recall that the phases of love-making were considered to have 47 different angels, each responsible for a developing phase. It was recommended that appropriate, if brief, acknowledgment should be paid to each angel in passing from one phase to the next—an activity suitable for what might be termed "centimeter" sex, as opposed to the 10-second sprinters.)

Such "angel-ology" does not imply a lack of spontaneity.[20] But it does see the highest pleasure as involving the mind as well as the perineum, and it has lessons for those who think that sexual functioning can safely be left to our instinctive drives and desires. Some people fondly believe that love-making has its own natural progressions that will work automatically in a reasonably satisfying manner. Yet doctors' clinics, marriage guidance clinics, and the divorce courts are full of examples of failed sexual cooperation, of impotence and frigidity.

The orgasm has sometimes been called the "white woman's burden," since failure to achieve it is thought to be shameful, carrying with it a stigma of inadequacy and insensitivity. This leads to a disparaging of the orgasm—it has been likened by some to an involuntary sneeze—and to an almost Victorian acceptance by many women of the uncompleted sexual act. This in turn results in a more and more one-sided masculine performance, and in a tendency to shut off—by excessive muscular tension—the early stirrings of erotic feeling, which experience has shown usually to be frustrated in these women. Erotic feelings take a lot of shutting off, and so there has to be a correspondingly vigilant creation of muscular overcontraction until the contractions become part and parcel of the character structure. Love-making, quite categorically, does not necessarily work properly just by the light of nature. Where "nature" is distorted by mis-use, there is likely to be a corresponding lack of lasting satisfaction.

SEXUAL PERCEPTION

It is possible to have the largest library of sexual information the literate world can produce and comprehensive access to the facilities required, and yet still misfire. Here again is the familiar story of the differences between knowing *how* and knowing *that*. Sexual performance is in no way different from any other skill in its ultimate dependence on practice rather than theory. The stage may be set: the date, the soft lights; the marriage, the desire; the adjuncts and the adjuvants; the reflexes that carry their rhythms from swamp and forest to the comfort of the civilized bedroom. Something is still needed. Civilized man needs to make his sexual experience new not every time but every moment of every time.

How is each sexual moment to be creatively different? How can two people avoid the traps into which their more stupid reflexes will lead them? In the language of the Alexander Principle, how can awareness of USE be adapted into a subtle instrument of sexual communication?

There are helpful parallels to be drawn between our approach to works of art and our engagement in love-making. A work of art, as distinguished from kitsch, is that to which one can return again and again, noticing new aspects, revising initial impressions, discovering intricacies and nuances.

Some very obvious parallels suggest themselves—as many people have noted—in the world of music. An immature listener may at first be able to pick out from a Beethoven symphony only certain melodic passages, rhythmic patterns, and dominant instruments.[21] As he grows more experienced, he will begin to notice variations in themes or patterns, including perhaps some inversions, abbreviated versions, or transposed sections; he will be able to concentrate on different instruments and follow their development through the piece or through extended passages. He will have sufficient patience to listen to each movement in its sequence, and to notice differences in moods.

As he becomes a more accomplished listener, he will be able to discern relationships between disparate sections, and he will have the heightened freedom that allows him to focus now on one, now on another aspect of rhythm, melody, harmony, and instrumentation, and perhaps to focus on several of these aspects at the same time. Eventually, he comes to know it so well that he can re-create it in his mind, criticize certain performances of it, anticipate its implications and possibilities. In spite of such sophistication, he may at times employ only a primitive perception, and focus merely on the melody and the rhythm, ignoring other aspects. Unlike less developed listeners, he has the option of returning to a more articulated and refined apprehension of the piece if he desires.

In discussing such a sensitive musical appreciator, I don't think that I need draw heavy-handed parallels with sex appreciation, except perhaps to point out that in sexual activity one is more an orchestra player, producing as well as listening to the sound, than a member of the audience; and that for many of us this will be about the most creative and artistic act we will engage in.

THE BACKGROUND TO SEXUAL ACTIVITY

Three parts of the body besides the sex organs need to be thought about during love-making, since all three areas may produce unhelpful tension. The three must be considered in different ways, for they can put the kibosh on sexual flow. They are: the muscles of the head and neck; the muscles of the chest and abdomen as they affect breathing; and the muscles of the lower back, pelvis, and thighs as they affect genital movement. (The arms and legs obviously can also become tense and mis-used in sexual activity; but, by and large, they will behave fairly well so long as the pelvis is free, and so long as the shoulders and the hip and knee joints actually move.)

To some extent, the tensions that arise in the head and neck region (Alexander's "primary control") have been considered. It may be helpful to look at the dystonic patterns that can form around the activity of breathing. Not only during sexual activity but in many other ways, breathing is inseparable from the handling of the emotional life of each of us.

The connection between sexual feeling and breathing has been frequently stressed before. Ancient Yoga disciplines prescribed complicated—and more or less impossible—regimes of taking in air through one nostril down to the genital area, where it was to be circulated around before being brought up to be expelled through the other nostril. Recently breathing techniques have again come into prominence with the work of Wilhelm Reich. I first encountered Reich's ideas in the United States in 1949, and was impressed then by his account of "muscle-armoring"—states of tension that prevent the full experience of sexuality.

Reich's account of the stages of the orgasm was masterly, but he sadly misfired in his concept of breathing. Lacking an adequate concept of USE, he laid down a number of muscular and breathing techniques that, after the first novelty wears off, are apt to leave basic dystonic patterns scarcely altered. The violence of his breathing and pelvic movements—although perhaps giving brief emotional release to some really frozen and unresponsive people—are too disconnected from everyday living to be of basic usefulness. The subtlety of Reich's written work does not seem to be matched by a corresponding subtlety in practice.

Indeed, similar breathing techniques are to be found even in the folklore of middle-class England. One crude way of inducing sexual feeling is to breathe out several times deeply from the upper chest to the genital area while at the same time slightly contracting the thighs and buttocks, and something like this was described by Reich. I am reliably informed by a splendid headmistress that in the girls' dorm at her school, they used to say "Come on, girls, let's URGE." This was accomplished by breathing out and contracting somewhat in the manner described, and it preceded Reich by at least twenty years. I would back Roedean against Reich, and no doubt the folklore of many other countries contains similar advice to young women and men.

I have no such esoteric advice to give; my advice is simply that one must learn not to fix the breathing through excessive or wrongly distributed muscle tension. If one is emotionally disturbed either by flaws in the sexual flow or by other matters, it is always helpful to try to introduce order into the sequence of breathing. It is important not to *start* to breathe in by a movement which raises the upper chest and breastbone, although this region will normally be raised a little at the *end* of breathing. It is helpful to learn to release tension in the shoulders and upper chest as you begin to *breathe out*—this is the only point in the breathing cycle at which upper-chest tensions can be released without upsetting the cycle. The more breathing can be thought of as an activity of the middle of the back, and of the back and sides of the abdomen, the less the opportunity for harmful tension.

HOW TO LIE DOWN

Sex manuals are filled with innumerable varieties of coital positions—sitting, standing, lying, kneeling, this way and that. But, by and large, most love-making involves at least one partner lying down, and usually one or the other's legs are going to be relatively straightened out at the hip joint.

It is interesting that, in the past, when people talked about evolution of the upright posture, they usually meant standing or sitting upright. Few animals except man can *lie* with their legs straightened out from the pelvis. We do not automatically know how to lie down properly with our legs out straight, any more than we know how to stand and sit upright properly. If there is to be an adequate and subtle adjustment of the pelvis and its muscles during coitus, we need to know more about a balanced resting position of the pelvis when we are lying down.

Lie down on your back (see Fig. 25), with your elbows out to the side and your knees pointing upward toward the ceiling. In this position there should be no arch in your back. It should be impossible to insert a hand between your lower back and the surface you are lying on. If in fact you are arching your back in this position, it will be due to two things. The front of your chest at its lowest point is being pushed forward too much and the whole chest cage needs to lie much flatter against the supporting surface, with the shoulder blades widening apart. The second, and more common reason is that your pelvis is arching forward toward your thighs. If you place your fingers about one and a half inches from your navel on either side and then run them down toward your pelvis, you will strike a jutting-out piece of the pelvis on each side. These "spines" of the pelvis, when you are arching your back, will be too close to the thighs. The buttocks need to be dropped slightly down and away from the middle of the back—this may be quite a big adjustment if you are very arched at rest—and in so doing the pelvic spines will drop slightly toward the abdominal cavity. If you keep your fingers on the spines as you make this movement, you may get the impression that the spines are separating from each other. The movement I have been describing—as will be apparent—is very much concerned in the approximation of genital surfaces. During coitus, such a movement by both men and women when accompanied by a slight buttock contraction will constitute the inward sexual connection, the slight releasing of tension the outward movement.

The composite movement of the pelvis forward, which involves slight flattening of the back, will also correspond to widening across the back of the chest that occurs when breath is taken in. The slight tilting back of the pelvis as the genitals are separated is accompanied by breathing out and by slight relaxation of vaginal musculature or of perineal musculature in the man.

The correction of an unduly arched pelvis and back is, of course, a much larger adjustment than the minuscule "plateau" movements of coitus. Given a range of movement from A to B, the resting position should be about halfway between A and B. If—as in the case of the arched back—the resting position is much closer to A than to B, then the potentiality for muscular relaxation and contraction, lengthening and shortening, is markedly limited. And if certain muscles around the pelvis are held almost permanently overcontracted, the scope for progressional movement is small.

The muscles that are usually found to be overcontracted are the buttock muscles themselves, plus the muscles of the front and inside of the upper thigh. When you are lying down as I have described, with the fingers on the spines of the pelvis, you may find that one side is higher (closer to the ceiling) than the other, or that one spine may be raised up closer to your chest than the other. If this is so, you will probably find that you are distributing your weight more along one side of your back than the other. It should be relatively easy to distribute the weight equally, although you may find as you do it that your head rotates to one side and will have to be rotated back if it is to be free.

MUSCULAR BLOCKS AND INTERFERENCES

Sexual activity, like breathing, is not "about" anything. It can of course be said that it is about producing children or pleasure one with another, just as breathing can be used for producing speech. But the basic processes of sex and breathing are not about anything. A process is going on and a process is something that you must let happen— not interfere with. There are no rules for the right way to engage in these processes—perhaps only rules for what not to do. In our moment-to-moment living, we too often make this mistake of *doing* some fixed thing, instead of engaging in some process; we *read, copulate, eat, speak,* instead of engaging in the *process* of reading, the *process* of copulation, the *process* of eating, the *process* of speaking.

As human beings, we are so constructed that we work best when we concern ourselves with process. When we are concerned with *ends* rather than *means*, our bodies don't function as well. The human organism is built for process operation, not for end-gaining.

As we engage in a process, something unexpected may happen and if we are not end-gaining, we can notice it and adjust ourselves to it. The psycho-mechanics of sex must learn not to interfere with processes and rhythms that arise and develop spontaneously; if there are to be new perceptions, it must learn to regulate without interference.

Interference takes place at two levels. At the gross mechanical level, postures that have been developed over many years will limit mobility either because the surrounding joints have become stiff with mis-use or because sexual leverages produce pain and cramp in already overtense muscles. It is not surprising that mis-used man has in recent years embarked on a variety of sexual practices that involve only a bare minimum of mechanical mobility. When the lower back, pelvis, and limbs can move freely, there is surely enough potential sexual experience to last several lifetimes.

At a more subtle level, muscular tension pattern of great complexity interferes with the quality of sensation that is fed back to the brain from the ongoing processes of muscular movement and contraction. The mechanisms of balanced sensitivity (which have already been touched on in the previous chapter) are likely to become blocked by tension, and any attempt to unblock a feeling of deadness by specific or movement is likely to fail. Under such circumstances, the capacity to give orders and directions to the main core structure—i.e., the head, neck, back, and breathing—is the quickest way to unblock a purely local tension. We have seen that a writer's cramp cannot be adequately treated by concentration on releasing the muscles of the wrist and hand; there must first be attention to the coordination of the neck and shoulder. In the same way, pelvic tensions—once they have become maldistributed—require a release of tension first in the neck and shoulders and then an improved use of the middle of the back and thorax.

Arthur K. was a pianist of fifty-two who had been married for three years but had never managed to consummate his marriage. He had previously been receiving psychotherapy, and he told me that his only experience of orgasm had been in his late teens, when he had been severely reproved for masturbating. He assured me that since that time there had been no sexual outlet, and that his psychotherapist blamed his deadness on his unsatisfactory early experience.

He had been referred to me primarily for treatment of a painful arm and shoulder, and it was several weeks before he admitted to his sexual problem. I had already begun to tackle with him the excessive and maldistributed tension patterns around his lower back and legs, and he was gradually learning to release some of the tension. He progressed to the point when I was able to show him a coordination of his lower back and pelvis in which his use became normally balanced. At this point he blurted out, "I can't do that, it makes me think of the sexual act."

I continued to familiarize him with the new coordination in the easy safety of my training conditions, and he arranged to see me the following week. When he returned, he told me an extraordinary story of returning home and seeing a nude photograph in one of the color magazines that aroused him greatly, to the point when he was able to consummate his marriage—history does not relate what his wife thought about it—and thereafter he had been able to repeat the experience.

Insight into the factors that led us in the past to set up a muscular defensive block will not necessarily untie muscular blocks which, over a period of years, have become incorporated into our whole basic manner of use. In this case, only after the blocks had been removed and the patient felt reassured and at ease in the unblocked state was he able to respond without blocking when he was away from me.

Stories like this one, which occur again and again in the re-educational situation, illustrate the fear people have of unusual feelings. Most muscular blocks and defenses were chosen for what seemed to be a good reason at the time: usually to avoid pain or rebuke (the so-called traumatic avoidance response), rather like the child who learns to call fire a "no-no" after being scared from it by being burned and by his parents' shouting. The ongoing sexual sensation of free movement and flowing can also become a "no-no," and the release of a tension that is blocking the flow may lead to anxiety—or tears, or laughter, or anger; anything to distract one's attention from the experience of releasing tension.

The patient with muscular blocks has to learn to disregard his usual body-construct. He has to learn not to construe his feelings as a "no-no." He can learn through the Alexander Principle to occupy his thinking with the projection of a new body-construct, which in its turn will feed back new sensations to his brain—sensations that will have no fear connotations.

SEXUAL DISORDERS

The late Joan Malleson wrote to me about the relevance she saw in this approach to such sexual tensions as vaginismus, another of the muscular blocks that can come to lead a life of its own, outside its place in the general muscular hierarchy. Similarly, a pre-existent muscular dystonia can lead to disorders like premature ejaculation and can be helped by a general reordering of the body-construct. Reordering is relevant not only to the actual timing and performance of a sexual act, but to the role that habit and compulsion play in the desire for sexual outlet, and in the mental states of preparation and "guilty longing" that occupy many people's thoughts to a greater or lesser degree. (A recent survey indicated that most young adults think about sex once every fifteen minutes.)

Many people never get to the point of attempting the sexual act. Even in our present "free society," shyness and loneliness abound. Much has been written about the tragedy of being "taken unprepared," but there is the even greater tragedy of being prepared but never allowing oneself to be taken. Some people seem to spend their time putting their money in the telephone box and going through all the work of dialing the number they want, but at the critical moment, when they have only to "press Button A" to get in contact, they press Button B to get their money back. Even when they can hear their own true love speaking at the other end, urging them to press Button A, their nerve fails and they press Button B again.

However free the social opportunities may seem, shyness and loneliness continue to be induced by muscular blocks and defenses that prevent the making and taking of opportunity.

FREEDOM IN THOUGHT

Alexander was dead before what the 1970s call "the permissive society" was upon us. But before the seventies his views on freedom had been often expressed: that *external* freedom to carry out certain actions (freedom *of* thought and action) is far less important than our own personal freedom *in* thought and action. He rightly saw that even when we have the most perfect conditions of environment, company, and cash, our happiness will still be determined by our capacity to think newly and freely. Such a capacity is limited by our manner of use.

It is a great improvement over times past that young (and old) people can now find easier sexual outlets without guilt, and without the feeling that someone will disapprove. The sexual drive is of basic strength. The human body is prodigal of sexual functioning. Not only are millions of spermatozoa made available for a task that one alone can complete, but some degree of sexual pleasure is available even to a severely sick person. The brain is claimed to be the last region of the body to die, but the gonads must run it a pretty close second. The sick man, the evil man, the old man do not easily lose their sexual pleasure.

I remember, when I was working as a house surgeon, being summoned out of bed to the private ward in the middle of the night by an elderly clergyman whose prostate had been removed and who found to his dismay that he could not obtain an erection. He was not himself, of course, and a few weeks later he must have blushed at the memory though he was pacified by my reassurance at the time. However, the incident does indicate how persistent the sexual urge is, and why moral codes and punishments have seemed necessary in the past to curb such a persistent urge, and why the individual may feel the social need to adopt blocking tactics.

Innumerable treatises have been written on moral philosophy, on free will and choice. Innumerable theologies have presented views on the good life. About heaven and abominations and the wrath to come. You would think that out of all this lot, somewhere someone would be able to give a young (or old) person really useful advice about whether or not, and when, to indulge in sexual activity. Ninety-five percent or more of all men masturbate or have masturbated at some time. A considerable number will be wondering in the future whether or not to masturbate. Dry textbooks of moral philosophy would surely become best-sellers if they genuinely considered this one sexual dilemma.

Perhaps I have an exaggerated view of its importance.

The English public school system—the one I know—insisted on little adolescent boys jumping out of bed at 7 A.M., and, at my particular establishment, pajamas had to be removed and there was a quick run down the stairs to an icy-cold shower where—observed by jeering older boys—a jet of cold water played over the anatomy. Now, it was an observable fact that most of the small adolescents were in a state of modified erection—modified, that is, by the icy dash. Indeed, one boy kept his father's large hunter watch by his bed and applied it to his genitals, in the hope of taking the impetus out of his tumescence before the embarrassing run was made. Many of the boys—such of them as one talked to—were plagued by guilt. Others made a thorough Portnoy of their situation, and one of them reckoned to achieve two orgasms—watched by an admiring group of friends—between the ringing of the bell for prayers and turning up spick-and-span in hall two minutes later for the benediction.

For what it is worth—and as the sympathetic recipient of countless "confessions" from worried patients—I have never seen anyone whose sexual apparatus was harmed in the process, nor do large-scale masturbators seem eventually to fail more than less frequent performers to achieve successful coitus. A few of them may lose the exploratory drive that the demand of an unsatisfied sexual urge would give them. And most of them are perpetually worried by the problem of "shall I, shan't I."

The only observation I can make about the morals of whether or not to have sex with or without a sexual partner, and when, is the phrase I culled from Professor Sparshott's excellent monograph, *An Enquiry into Goodness*.[22] He puts forward the view that "to say that a thing is good is to say that it is such as to satisfy the desires and needs of the person or persons concerned." It takes Professor Sparshott a whole book to sort out the implications of this one sentence; but the advantage of the view is that it does refer to other people as well as to oneself and it can also include oneself not only as one is today, here and now, but oneself in a month's time, a year's time, five years' time. Oneself at a later date is very much one of the persons whose needs have to be thought about; obviously, oneself in five years' time with syphilis or a genital stricture or a fatherless child has to be considered, as also has oneself with a "frozen" insensitive sexual orientation owing to overcaution and timidity. As with most things, though—unfortunately—we don't know till we have tried. One can try to avoid making the same mistakes too often, and one can try to avoid being frightened off by one or two bad experiences with unsuitable people. One can avoid labeling oneself homosexual after one or two disastrous fumblings with the opposite sex or after one or two enjoyable experiences with the same sex. Perhaps one can learn from a knowledge of the Alexander Principle that if the USE of certain partners is muddled and disorganized, they may be pleasant companions over a short period, but the unpleasant and difficult habits that are already observable in their USE will make life miserable for both of them over a long period. On the obverse side of the coin, you may perhaps find it easier to salvage something out of a relationship that still has much to commend it *if you can learn to attend to your own mis-use patterns,* or if this does not help, you may find that a more stable manner of use will give you the courage to make or take the break.

Part II

PRACTICE

CHAPTER 7

Teaching the Principle

Some come in hope and others come in fear
Diverse in shape the multitude appear.

—POPE

Alexander instruction is, at first, an individual matter, one to one. Unless it is detailed, it is nothing. The Alexander teacher will have his subjects with him between half an hour and an hour, during which time there is a continuously absorbing preoccupation with the development of new USE. For most people this will involve at least fifteen sessions. For many it will involve very many more. Relatively stereotyped procedures of physiotherapy or mainpulation may produce a greater turnover of patients, and with less effort. This can never be so with Alexander instruction. A teacher can deal with only a comparatively small number of people in a working day.

Learning a better general USE is no different in kind from learning any other specific skill, but with or without a teacher it will involve working at two simultaneous levels —a mental "labeling" level, and a psychophysical "experiencing" level. To illustrate these two levels, let us think of someone who is blindfolded and trying to make out what an object (A) in front of him is:

A

Object in
Outside World

Sense

Receptors

B

Raw Experience ⟶

C

Label

His sense receptors will tell him first that it is heavy, smooth, cold, rounded, etc.; he is getting from the senses a "raw" unformulated experience (B). Very soon he will think he recognizes it, and may give it a label (C): a "jug," perhaps.

The labeling process, C, involves discrimination and recognition according to what we know already about jugs, etc. The label is *not* the experience; the word is not the object. The two levels must not be confused, although one leads to the other.

An animal in the forest has, presumably, a fairly simple labeling process. If it is a monkey which is in ever-present danger of being eaten by a tiger, the important thing is to be able to detect the tiger before it actually arrives. A scent on the breeze, level B, is associated in a flash with the thought, level C, of a tiger, and this stimulates an immediate response—probably shinning up a tree with all the other monkeys. However, it would be useless for a well-meaning tiger to shout "Look out! Tiger, tiger!" because the verbal label "tiger" would mean nothing, whereas the scent on the breeze would mean everything. Words and ideas by themselves are not a sufficient form of education in anything that involves the senses, and they can only become effective when they have been linked to a raw experience by a learning procedure. Thus, in time, a monkey might be trained to get up a tree whenever someone shouted "Tiger!"

If a new USE is to be learned, it is necessary for many new experiences of USE, level B, to come to be associated with new labels, level C; and the new labels will, in time, come to induce the improved USE. In human beings, the new USE label cannot be as simple as that of the conditioned animal; but a simple association must first be set up between the names of various USES and the actual USES themselves. A grammar of the body has to be learned, a grammar not to be triggered into action by some external cry of "Tiger, tiger," but by being projected personally as and when one wishes.

THE GRAMMAR OF THE BODY

An electrical recording that has been obtained from muscles during re-education illustrates procedure clearly. It shows the neck muscles being trained to release while at the same time the patient repeats to himself a verbal direction "neck release." At first, there is initial tension in the neck; then the tension becomes momentarily less, but returns as soon as the teacher stops his gentle adjustment of the head. The improved balance is obtained sooner when the teacher continues again, but still the tension returns when the teacher stops his adjustment. Later, the patient is able to maintain the state of lessened tension and, in time, will be able to evoke this state simply by running over the "orders."

A sequence of such verbal directions is taught while

a better tensional balance is obtained all over the body; the sequence is designed to scan the body in serial order, much as a television camera scans its object or as one scans a telephone directory in search of a number. The sequence of directions then provides a model with both spatial and temporal coordinates. Such a sequence fulfills the function of checking the development of too much tension and of restoring a resting state when it has been disturbed. If the sequence is kept in mind during performance, it will insure that deviations from the resting state are not excessive.

END-GAINING

A great many people prepare for action by creating unnecessary muscle tension. One of the most interesting and original ideas Alexander put forward to explain such tension was his concept of "end-gaining." In order to understand what takes place in an Alexander lesson, it is essential that this concept should be understood.

Briefly, end-gaining means the habit of working for ends, targets, goals, results without considering the means; without insuring that the means we use won't produce too many harmful by-products.

End-gaining shows itself in the form of overquick and overenergetic reactions. Targets—when we live by the end-gaining principle—have to be reached as soon as possible, so that yet another target can be achieved; not only big goals and achievements, but small actions like turning the tap on, picking things up, swallowing food, or interrupting people.

In end-gaining terms, a successful life is one that achieves more and more goals, and the devil take the hindmost. These goals may either be personally selected or they may be the ones that we have been encouraged by our society to select;

but whether they be the goals of the "organization man" or the lonely pioneer, end-gaining implies that proper consideration is not being given to the USE involved in gaining the end.

This concept of end-gaining was taken up with avidity by John Dewey, the American educational philosopher, who saw it as a way children could become more interested in what they were doing than in the pat on the back that they hoped to get from exam success or from being top of the form. It was also taken up by Aldous Huxley, who wrote in *Ends and Means:*

> We are all, in Alexander's phrase, end-gainers. We have goals towards which we hasten without ever considering the means whereby we can best achieve our purpose. The ideal man is one who is non-attached. All education must ultimately aim at producing non-attachment.

Modern interest in meditation has led some writers to see in Alexander's end-gaining the same fault that they themselves are trying to eliminate. For this reason some of the writing about Alexander has had a mystical flavor, not to say sentimentality. Experiences that can come from what Alexander called "inhibiting" such end-gaining have been seen by some people as more important than any of the other effects of good USE.

INHIBITING

"Inhibiting," as Alexander suggested it, is not to be confused with repression and unresponsiveness as understood by the psychotherapists. Alexander had a fairly simple stimulus-response psychology, and his behavior diagram went something like this:

He saw, rightly, that end-gaining was a reflex action which tended to by-pass the reasoning brain and that most end-gainers are reacting automatically on an input-output basis, so that activity is directed toward satisfying the input as soon as possible, whether or not the habitual way of doing it is appropriate. Accordingly, he insisted that on the receipt of a stimulus there must be an "inhibition" of the immediate muscular response, so that by "throughput" there could be adequate preparation for the succeeding activity. Such inhibition became a cornerstone of his re-educational methods.

Unfortunately, the person who refuses to react and to register sensations may find himself in a state of disorientation. Like the philosopher who stood on a riverbank watching someone drown while he tried to decide whether human life was valuable, the use of inhibition has led some Alexander adherents in the past to a state of passivity, in which they prefer not to respond at all for fear their dystonic patterns should reappear. Such "sensory deprivation," which may come from overzealous inhibition, must clearly be used with care. However, this snag disappears if the period of inhibition is seen merely as a stage of preparatory choice in which the eventual muscular USE can be decided on—a stage that leads on to activity or to a state of freedom while at rest.

THE ALEXANDER TECHNIQUE

The Alexander technique is, briefly, a method of showing people how they are mis-using their bodies and how they can prevent such mis-use, whether it be at rest or during activity. This information about USE is conveyed by manual adjustment on the part of the teacher, and it involves learning of a new mental pattern in the form of a sequence of words which are taught to the patient or pupil, and which he learns to associate with the new muscular use he is being taught by the manual adjustment. He learns to project this new pattern to himself not only while he is being taught but when he is on his own.

This procedure is *not* a method of manipulation in which the subject is a passive recipient. It is a method by which he is taught to work on himself to prevent his recurrent habits of mis-use, and by which he can learn to build up a new use structure.

It is *not* a form of hypnosis, by which the mind is conditioned to obey commands some other person has planted there. It could perhaps be described, in its initial phase, as a deconditioning, since it aims to teach the pupil to recognize when he is making faulty tension. It is not akin to the deconditioning procedures of behavior therapy, in which, say, the tension of a writer's cramp is punished by giving an electric shock every time the pen is held wrongly. Instead, it involves a conscious attention and learning by the patient. No adjustments are considered useful unless they can be built up into a new body-construct, to be used consciously by the patient afterward.

It is *not* a form of relaxation therapy. Certainly the pupil will learn to release tension that was previously unconscious, but in all probability he will be expected to replace the unnecessary tension by additional work in other muscle groups which previously had been underemployed. Many people, for example, who have picked up the bad habit of slumping and crossing their knees will have to put more work into their lower back and thighs if they are to release excessive tension they have been making in their neck and shoulders. The overtension of the neck and shoulders will be replaced by more tone in the lower back and thighs; but, of course, we all have individual patterns with different arrangements of wrong muscle tension that need to be redistributed.

DEFECTIVE AWARENESS

It might be thought that once a proper USE diagnosis has been made, learning should be easy. Assuming that people are interfering with their USE in a certain way, then, one would hope, all that is necessary is to show them what is right and get them to practice it.

Unfortunately the problem is not so easy. When people have grown accustomed to a certain manner of use—no matter how twisted or crooked—it will have come to feel "right" to them even though it may also be producing pain and inefficiency and clumsiness. Our sense of "rightness" is a very precious possession to most of us—it is, after all, the outcome of our experience of living to date. Our whole nature is bound up with the substratum of muscle tone that underlies our USE, and a sense of the space coordination of our postural system pervades all our behavior. We *are* our posture.

The moment we try to carry out a basic re-education of USE, we very rapidly run up against our attachment to the old feeling of ourselves. We can be shown in detail what are our defects, and most of us will readily admit that they need altering. Nonetheless, very many people try to correct their mis-uses by deliberately taking up some new position that they think is what is now required. In the process they will only create yet another set of dystonic patterns. Not long afterward, they will revert to the old habitual pattern, particularly when they start to move. It may be recalled that out of my group of 108 young men (Chapter 2), only 11 were able to alter their habits at will, and then only at the immediate moment of supervision.

THE ALEXANDER LESSON

Alexander himself has described how he managed to teach himself a new body-construct, and to associate it with a new manner of use. But this is a laborious business on one's own, and, in common with most skills, it is all far easier with the help of a good teacher.

It may be of assistance to describe an Alexander lesson, although of course each teacher will have worked out his own ways of presenting the necessary information as clearly as he can.

An initial examination by the teacher indicates that there are certain forms of wrong USE which are deeply established. These uses show themselves in the disposition and alignment of the bones of the vertebral column and limbs, and in a disposition to react with the muscles in certain habitual ways. It is taken for granted that the pupil has been sufficiently persuaded by the diagnosis to accept the type of instruction which is being given.

The pupil will be asked to lie down on a fairly hard surface—the usual medical or physiotherapy couch is a good height. The head will need about one inch of firm support under it, although up to three inches may be needed if the hump has become fixed and very bent forward. The pupil will be told not to do anything—in other words to "inhibit" any reflex movement that tends to take place when he is handled or moved.

The teacher places both his hands at the sides of the neck and asks the pupil to say to himself the words "NECK FREE, HEAD FORWARD AND OUT." He perhaps explains that "FORWARD" means the opposite of pushing the skull back into the support under the head, and that "OUT" is the opposite of retracting the skull, like a tortoise, into the hump and the chest. (When the pupil is standing or sitting, the instruction may be "FORWARD AND UP," which amounts to the same thing.) The teacher repeats these words as he gently adjusts the head in such a way as to release neck tensions that are preventing it from going forward and out. These neck tensions will be manifold and different in each one of us. The neck X-rays in Plate 2 show just a few of the sorts of contortions into which we can get our necks and heads. To some extent such contortions are gently corrected as the teacher takes the head forward and out. Obviously the tensions and distortions of a lifetime won't come undone in one magic moment; and, equally obvious, the somewhat improved balance that is initially attained in this way cannot be taken to be the one final and right answer. Over a period of days and weeks, the pupil will gradually become familiarized with an improving and changing use of the head and neck.

This familiarization with a new USE would not, in itself, be of much value. It is also necessary for the pupil to learn how to maintain the improving use when he starts to react.

At first, the teacher will present only quite a small stimulus. He might suggest that the pupil should let him turn his head by rotating it to one side. Many people—most people, in fact—when such a movement is suggested, are not able to let the teacher carry out the movement for them, but start to do it themselves. The pupil will therefore be told not to do the movement, but, in Alexander phraseology, to "inhibit." In terms of our "Input-Throughput-Output" diagram (page 171), when a stimulus is received, it is necessary not to respond with an immediate muscular output, but instead to engage in throughput—that is to say, "Head forward and out." While these words are projected, and provided the pupil "inhibits" the movement the teacher says he is going to carry out, it becomes possible to detect just when tension is created in the neck and around the head and throat.

At some point in this procedure, the teacher will have emphasized the importance of the direction "NECK FREE," so that the pupil will come to associate with the direction "NECK FREE, HEAD FORWARD AND OUT" not only a spatial positioning of the skull in relation to the chest and hump, but also a releasing of neck and throat tensions that have become apparent.

When the teacher adjusts the head, he is able to release quite a lot of tension in the neck and hump; but the pupil will also notice that some slight force is being exerted on the back of the chest and the lower back. When this occurs, the teacher gives the verbal direction "BACK LENGTHEN AND WIDEN," while in various and devious ways he achieves such a coordination. In lengthening the back, he will be at pains not to produce an undue arch in the middle of the back, and, indeed, by adjustment of the chest and pelvis, he will see to it that the lower back becomes almost completely flat on the couch. As he continues with this procedure, he will insist that the new verbal direction should be in the right order. If, as he adjusts the lower back, the pupil should stiffen his neck, the teacher will insist that the pupil should emphasize to himself, "Head forward and up," until it is clearly perceived, and then add on to it the direction to the back, "Lengthen and widen." With his hands the teacher will repeat the muscular experiences in the right order—a task that sounds complex when written down in this way, but fairly obvious in practice when undertaken by a skilled instructor.

There are many more such "orders" to be added to the new body grammar. The teacher may now say that he wishes to move one of the legs so that the hip flexes and the knee points toward the ceiling. He will again insist on the pupil "inhibiting" any doing of the movement, and he will ask him to continue to project the orders to the neck, head, and back, and to add to them such an order as "KNEE OUT OF THE HIP," or perhaps "HIP FREE," or "KNEE TO THE CEIL-

ING." (There is no right or wrong about the verbal phrasing of such orders, but merely a sequence in which it is best to give attention to the body.*)

The point at which teachers will tackle the shoulders and arms may vary. I personally think they should very soon be linked up with the instruction to free the neck, since many neck and chest tensions will not release until the whole shoulder girdle—comprising the shoulder blade and collarbone—is adjusted. I usually suggest the order "SHOULDER RELEASE AND WIDEN." Since this is always a dramatic adjustment at first, I find it helpful to do it in the first session. A most obvious feeling of bodily readjustment usually takes place, and even the dimmest of patients (kinesthetically, that is) will usually notice when one shoulder is placed two inches wider and lower than the other. And since the trapezius muscle goes from the back of the head, down the side of the neck, into the shoulder girdle, it is possible to give the subject an easy and obvious demonstration. Unless he thinks of his head going "forward and out" as his shoulder is adjusted, his head will simply pull down with the shoulder because of the trapezius contraction. Most people, during this procedure, realize that by giving careful attention (in the form of the verbal "orders") they can maintain an improved head-neck-shoulder balance.

But again, the varieties of shoulder use are considerable, and all that can be looked for is a gradual transition to a physiological norm. It is explained again and again to the

* Professor G. E. Coghill, whose *Anatomy and the Problems of Behaviour* was considered a classic in its time by such people as LeGros Clark and J. Z. Young, explained that the correct sequence was cephalo-caudal, from head to tail. His book, along with Judson Herrick's biography, *G. E. Coghill: Naturalist and Philosopher* (Chicago, 1949), is useful reading, since he gave wholehearted backing to Alexander. I touched on Coghill's account of sequential ordering in an article in the *Lancet* (September, 1955, p. 659).

patient that what he is learning is a neutral "resting position" of balance for the various parts of his body—rather like the "neutral" of a car to which one can return after one has been in gear. And it is stressed throughout that for any given position or activity there is a due amount of muscle tension necessary. More muscle work will be needed for sitting than lying—more work in lifting a hammer than a toothbrush—but the increase in muscular activity has to be undertaken on a general and not a local basis. Increased forearm work should not be produced in a way that involves hunching the shoulders and tensing one side of the neck. Lack of interference with Alexander's "primary control" of the head and neck is taken to be of utmost importance at rest and during activity.

It is unlikely that in the initial session or two much more can be done than to familiarize the patient with the words of his new body grammar, and to get him used to being handled in a certain way and a certain sequence. The impact of this whole procedure is considerable, and most people realize that they are being asked to set about things in a way that is quite novel and individual to them. I have had young people describe to me the immense impression such "lessons" made upon them in their early childhood, and the feeling of security and individual attention they remember.

Indeed, it is on this fundamental basis of practical attention and instruction that the patient/pupil will eventually be prepared to release more deep-seated and unconscious tension patterns. It can be frightening to surrender a familiar sense of balance to someone, and most of us have a multitude of tricks of "muscle-armoring" by which we defend ourselves from contact we fear to be harmful. This goes for seemingly quite normal people, as well as for those who are in a state of apprehension or distress. A well-constructed Alexander lesson will have the effect of making the subject feel not that he is being got at but that both he and the teacher are learning together how to sort out the mis-use problems. There is not one master key—Alexander's primary control—that will unlock the prison, but rather there is a key blank, out of which, by using the Alexander Principle, an individual key may be constructed; a key that can be used to unlock our unnecessary defenses and to open up a way of dealing with future buffetings. Life will always buffet us if we are to live fully.

SITTING AND STANDING

Many Alexander teachers prefer to begin instruction in the active situations of sitting and standing. The subject may be asked to take up a standing position, and it will be emphasized that he is not to "do" the new body pattern, but simply to project it to himself. He must never "do" the orders; he must just think them. It will be explained that such "ordering" is always a "pre-" activity; that when we receive an outside stimulus (or an inside one) we are all likely to react with preparatory tension. We are likely to get "set" in preparation for what we are going to do, and such an anticipatory preset usually triggers us off into far too much effort when we initiate a movement.*

When the subject is standing quite still, the teacher will

---

* A body sliding along a surface is restricted by *friction*, but to start moving along a surface, it is necessary to overcome what engineers call "stiction"; to get a car moving, we have to use low gears to overcome the initial inertia. In much the same way, our joints exhibit this property of "stiction." They tend to get relatively stuck when they are held still and fixed for a time, and an extra effort may be needed to initiate movement. The solution to this is not to allow ourselves to become fixed when we are at rest, and to let out the clutch slowly when we get up from a chair or in any other movement involving change of position.

obtain as good a preset as he can by his gentle manual adjustment. He will then ask the subject to project the new body pattern continuously as the knees are bent forward to sit down. At first, this is an unfamiliar experience in which the usual balance may seem to be alarmingly upset. In time, however, it becomes familiar, and in this specific situation of sitting down and standing up much insight can be gained into faulty tensional habits and into the maintenance of the new pattern under stress. Likewise, when the subject is in the sitting position, small movements of the trunk backward and forward from the hip joint (while maintaining the improved direction of head, neck, and back) can be used to teach him how to attend to his USE. It should be explained that in such activities, the subject is not learning a correct way to sit and stand but how to attend to his USE and prevent unnecessary tension.

Alexander frequently wrote of a "position of mechanical advantage." An easy way to achieve this is to slide your back down a wall, at the same time putting your knees away and flexing your pelvis so that the whole back is flat against the wall. If the entire spine from head to pelvis is now kept lengthening, it can be inclined forward but with the buttocks still touching the wall (Fig. 24). In this situation, the directions are "Head forward and up, back lengthen and widen, knees forward and apart," and, in addition, the neck can be directed to lengthen "up and back" and the lumbar spine likewise up and back. The shoulder blades will now move around the chest more easily, so that when the back is returned to the wall, they remain relatively widened apart. And it will be seen (Plate 18) that the unduly arched back has now become straighter.

Throughout this maneuver, attention is given to inhibiting and projecting the new body-construct, which includes the orders to the knees and ankles and elbows and hands. Such detailed attention leads to a heightened awareness of the

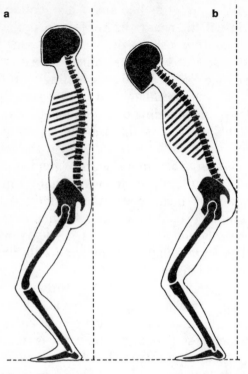

figure 24

coordination of the whole body. Most subjects will experience an exhilarating feeling of lightness and "upness" in their bodies as they begin thus to engage their minds.*

THE ALEXANDER TEACHER

Alexander teachers, naturally, vary in their approaches, but, unlike teachers in other teaching situations, they all

---

* Many mystical experiences include an "up" component (Marghanita Laski, *Ecstasy* [Grosset Press, 1961]).

have one goal in common: to obey their own educational demands if they are to influence their pupils. It is for this reason that the training of Alexander teachers has always first been aimed at improving their own USE to a point where they have not only a high standard but one they can sustain when they are under full teaching pressure. This does not mean that in order to teach well it is necessary for the teacher to be in some ineffable state of "directive lightness." At the other end of the scale, the teaching can never become automatic and rule-of-thumb, since each pupil presents his own personal problems and difficulties.

A detached form of teaching which relies on a pedagogic, professorial, didactic attitude is simply not possible. It is intensely boring if during a lesson the teacher gives the impression that he is seeking to expound a thesis or prove a case, and makes the pupil feel he is being reproved if his attention wanders or if for a moment he disagrees.

The pupil also must realize that the learning process involves a most detailed attention on his part. Since his organism is being "re-calibrated," and brought back to true, he will eventually need to give attention to his USE all day long. Not only will he become freer while interacting with the outside world, but he will know how to return to a balanced state of rest after that interaction. Both he and his teacher can never forget what a tall order it is to ask him to disobey habit.

It follows that during a training program various emotions may be transferred to the teacher. There is often an initial honeymoon period of great pleasure in having discovered something that not only explains previous troubles but that also offers a solution. Some people continue their happy honeymoon into a long and successful marriage with the new idea and practices. But for many—and probably most—people there are bound to be breakdown periods that lead to a certain amount of depression and to a feeling of dissatisfaction that a given Alexander teacher is not being clear or helpful enough. Also, to see oneself as one really is must usually involve some cutting down on, or alteration in, outside commitments, at least for a time. Few people can expect to make big changes in themselves without experiencing periods of anxiety and depression, and they may find that they are not able to meet the need and challenge of the Alexander Principle without abandoning—temporarily, at least—the effort to pursue some other relationship. Added to this, most people at first feel slightly stupid with their new USE, because the components have not yet been incorporated into familiar sequential rhythms. Ease comes from a feeling of ongoing sequence—we can all remember our difficulties in first learning to drive or ski. The new Alexander USE has at the outset no clear place in our sequential organization. As, however, the patterns become incorporated into newly timed sequences, we get a feeling of ease and a motivation to use the new patterns—ease that at first can only be experienced when the teacher is giving us help. The enjoyable feeling of "lightness" that comes after working with a good teacher is in the beginning evanescent. If there is not to be an undue dependence on the teacher who can give us this "lightness"—and, with such dependence, all the concomitant problems of the transference situation—then the pupil must learn to work independently.

At present the majority of Alexander pupils are adults and adolescents who have found their way to a teacher, either through the guidance of their doctors or educational friends or simply by word of mouth. They form an immensely variegated cross-section of the population, and their problems are equally variegated. There can be no one correct way to learn the Principle; each will find his own way on the basis of his education and Alexander instruction.

CHAPTER 8

Learning the Principle

Here are a series of questions by a pupil, or prospective pupil, and answers from an Alexander teacher.

Just what sort of work am I expected to do on my own in order to achieve a balanced regulation of my body?

The Alexander technique aims to teach a pupil to associate a new sequence of thought with a new manner of using the body. You may already have found that when you run over the new sequence of thought you are aware of much unnecessary tension at rest, and unnecessary pressure during movement.

That sounds fine, but I don't seem to have much time or inclination to think about this sort of thing. I realize that I need to alter my old habits, but where am I to begin?

The situations that in the majority of people produce

muscle tension, and most frequently take them away from a balanced resting state, are:

a. Talking to other people, especially to people you know well, particularly when your job or life situation requires you to establish rapport with them.

b. The stimulus of handling familiar objects around you —the toothbrush, doorknob, articles of clothing, typewriter, gear handle, piano, food, and indeed the whole range of biological activities, from swallowing to excreting.

c. The commitments in which you are already engaged: e.g., the tennis player who plays on a team, the office boy who has to be obsequious, the business executive who feels he has to adopt a very forceful attitude, the dancer or physical education teacher who has to make movements that involve maldistributed tension, the teacher who has to fit teaching to a curriculum and get things done in a certain time.

d. The emotional gusts: waves of irritation, fear, sexual excitement, crying and sentimental eye-moistening, depression, suspicion, excitability.

e. Obsessional repetitive mental states: daydreaming, recurrent tunes in the head, self-conversation, etc. Such states occur as a background to tension that is already present, and the attempt to control them may lead to further tension.

f. Excessive desire for smoking, drinking, eating chocolates. It is not suggested that such things are harmful in moderation, but many people find themselves in a state of tension and conflict for which these are a poor form of palliation.

g. Fatigue: after making excessive tension there is a temptation to collapse and "slump." It is a mistake to slump in a chair—far better to lie horizontally if one is tired.

h. The feeling of unfamiliarity with the new conditions: feeling, for example, "stuck-up" or different when employing the new body-construct.

i. Rush: the need (or imagined need) to get things done quickly.

j. Frustration: civilization usually implies delay between desire and satisfaction, and under these conditions tension may mount up unless one consciously regulates it.

But how am I expected to alter these habits?

In your lessons so far, you will have realized the importance of inhibiting—"stopping off"—an immediate reaction to the stimuli which your teacher has given you. You will have found that unless you inhibit the stimulus, say, of sitting down or standing up, you react in the tense and distorted way that it is necessary to change. But you will have found that by inhibiting and employing the new form of "direction," you can usually prevent this happening. In the same way, it should now be possible for you to check your immediate reaction to many of the situations outlined above; and even if you find it impossible to maintain the improved tension balance, you are at any rate aware that it is desirable, and are able to return to a balanced resting equilibrium when the immediate stress is over.

Practical questions that many people raise at this point are:

Am I expected to think of this all day long?

In the beginning stages, it is most unlikely that you will be able to work at it all day long. Start with the simplest activities, and set aside special periods when you work at this and this only. There are, in addition, hours during the day when one must perforce keep still in one place—e.g., waiting for a bus—and many other times when overt activity is prevented or frustrated.

How, then, am I to work in these special periods?

You will probably have learned from your lessons that "realization" is more important than "trying." Intense concentration for short periods will not produce a lasting change in your manner of use, and the whole aim of your training has been that you should employ a balanced regulation all day long; but it is nevertheless a good idea to make a habit of working for short periods in the following way:

a. Find a place where you are not likely to be disturbed, and where, if necessary, you can lie down on the floor with a book under your head.

b. Lying down with a book under your head and with your knees pointing to the ceiling, decide consciously to keep quite still, and to inhibit reacting to stimuli; i.e., don't wriggle or scatch, and don't follow irrelevant patterns of thought. Give yourself the following verbal directions:

(i) "Neck release, head forward and up." As you give this sequence of thought, at first you will not "realize" what the direction means, but as you continue you will begin to associate it with an awareness that you may previously have had either when working well on yourself or during a lesson. By "awareness" is meant what should be a normal sense of "being in yourself," as opposed to the state of mind-body split that is so often present in adults, if not in children.

(ii) While you are still preserving by direction this awareness of the head and neck—an awareness in which your verbal order will be part and parcel of the actual perception as the organizing component of it—add on the verbal direction "Lengthen and widen your back." Your lessons will already have made you familiar with the meaning of this phrase, and it is likely that fresh meaning and fresh simplification will accrue as you run over the sequence to yourself. For example, you may realize the whole of the back as lengthening in one unit instead of thinking of the upper back as separate from the lower back; or perhaps you may suddenly notice that widening the back includes releasing the shoulder blade and upper arm. At this point, your interest in the new realization may have caused you to "lose" the head direction, and it will be necessary to reinforce it before returning to the lengthening and widening direction.

(iii) The process of adding together the direction to the head and the direction to the back may take several minutes or even longer: indeed, if it seems to take less time, you almost certainly have been making a muscular change by direct movement, instead of sticking to realizing the meaning of the orders. Remember that in this process we do not move our bodies in the same way as when we pick up an external object—a brush or a pen or a pail. To move our forearm is not the same as to move a spoon. Moving ourselves and bits of ourselves—as opposed to moving external objects—is always a question of allowing movement to take place, rather than of picking up and putting down somewhere else. Allowing the movement, say, of an arm will involve a total general awareness of the body; the active process involved in this particular movement is small compared with the active process of awareness that is going on in the whole of the body all of the time. Similarly, a movement of standing up after sitting down—a movement which involves mainly a leg adjustment—does not require only the leg activity, but primarily a maintenance of the awareness of the rest of the body while allowing the necessary leg movement to take place.

I am not clear what is meant by "ordering." I have not met anything quite like this in any other medical or teaching approach.

During an Alexander lesson two things are involved. The first is a gentle adjustment of the pupil—manually—by the teacher, to coax mis-used muscles into a better coordination. Secondly, the pupil (or patient, in a medical context) has to play his part in the proceedings by consciously projecting to himself a sequence of thought that matches closely the occurrences which his teacher is inducing in his musculature.

For most people this will be a totally novel undertaking. Behavior therapists have modes of muscle training, with punishments and rewards, but these are not the same. Message techniques, stroking techniques, body contact techniques likewise involve close contact between therapist and patient. Alexander's concept of "ordering" is quite different from any of these. It demands a minutely sensitive attention on the part of the pupil to the setting up of a new ordered structure in his body: *ordered* in the sense of being consciously projected as a command to the muscles, and *ordered* in the sense of giving sequential attention to the body in a certain 1, 2, 3, 4, 5, etc., order.

It is perhaps a play on words to speak of "ordering" in two senses—getting the muscles to react in the right *order* and giving *orders* to oneself. For this reason it is perhaps better to talk of giving "directions" to oneself. Whatever the activity is called, the pupil can learn an actual formal construction of words, which he learns to link on to the new desired USE, until, in time, the new verbal pattern can be "directed," "projected," "thought," in such a way as to bring the body into the desired state of balance.

Each patient will make his own method of "directing," which, with or without the help of a teacher, he can gradually learn to link up with the new desired USE structure.

When I was thinking about it yesterday, I noticed certain muscular changes taking place. You have told me I should

*be wary of trusting my feeling, and also that I should not
"do." Was I "doing" this muscular change I felt? In fact, was
I working the wrong way?*

If you were "ordering," it is possible that changes did take
place. Most people, however, when they notice such things
beginning to happen, stop "ordering" and get interested in
helping the changes by "doing." When you notice something
beginning to happen, it is more important than ever to
"think" and not to "do." However, if you move after having
"ordered" for quite a long time, muscular overtension will
release as you move, provided you continue ordering at the
same time. In other words, the directions you have learned
to give yourself affect the "preset" (the preparatory tension)
in your muscles.

Does it help if I visualize what you are teaching me?

No. The kinesthetic (muscular) sense is separate from
the visual sense. Visual imagery, which is almost certainly
associated with old, wrong muscular sensations, is likely to
lead to confusion between the old muscular sensations and
the new ones you have to learn. It is far safer to use a brand-
new symbolism to link up with the improved new kinesthetic
sense—a new "body-construct" made up of the body grammar that you have learned.

*Will you explain more clearly what you mean by "body-
construct"?*

In the past there have been many terms suggested for the
mental model we have of ourselves. In 1911, Henry Head
used the term "postural model," and wrote: "By means of
a perpetual alteration in posture, we are always building up
a postural model of ourselves which constantly changes." He
also spoke of "body memory," which modifies our perceptions at an unconscious level, so that our spatial consciousness is always bound to be influenced by what has happened
before.

The term "body image" was used by Schilder to include in one label the visual, mental, and memory images we may have of our bodies. Macdonald Critchley used the term in a similar way, and for many years neurophysiologists have sketched out a "homunculus"—a little-man image in the brain cortex—which is taken to represent various areas of the body. The term "body concept" has been used in reference to people who think that they are too tall or too short or that their breasts are too large or their bottoms too big.

Other writers have spoken of the "body percept," by which they mean the momentary perceptions we may have of our body at any given time, irrespective of the construction we may put upon perceptions, or of the mental factors that led us to obtain a particular perception.

For many reasons I prefer "body-construct," a term that implies not only the way we construe things but also the way we construct our responses and organize outside things so that they will appear the way we want them to be. Such a "body-construct" produces (and is based on) our habitual USE of our bodies, and it forms the background to our perceptions.

More often than not, once we are set and readied for a given course of action, it is impossible to think of doing anything else. Our preparatory "set" affects our observations so that we see everything in conformity to it. We all have had the experience, when waiting to carry out some activity, of being triggered off into action by a quite inappropriate stimulus, some accidental resemblance to the configuration that we are waiting for, or, when we are very strung up, something that bears no resemblance to it whatever. If we are to check such reactions and only release our response when the time is right, we must have control over our preparatory state. Our subjective experience of this preparatory state is what I understand by our "body-construct."

Does this mean that the new "body-construct" will eventually become unconscious?

No. A human being is not a one-way system, passively reacting on a stimulus-response basis according to previous conditioning. We search out from our surroundings the stimuli that we would prefer to perceive. We don't sit around waiting to salivate when a dinner gong may ring; we are constantly concerned with the "organization of preferred perceptions." These preferences make up the "body-construct" and are embedded in our habitual resting state. The organization of our preferred perceptions has its basis in the use of our muscles, whether they are used in posture, movement, or communication.

Such preferences are usually at an unchosen, unconscious level; our characteristic preferences are embodied in our muscular tension patterns. The Alexander Principle suggests that our "body-construct" must be used consciously and that this will involve us in "inhibiting" our habitual responses.

The repeated use of inhibiting and projecting a conscious body-construct would be an impossibility in everyday life unless some degree of amalgamative learning had taken place. At first, the new details of muscular USE may have to be "thought out"; but in time, this becomes a state of "thoughtful movement," rather than of "thought-out action."

To understand how this happens, let us consider the learning of some special skill like driving a car. The way in which driving a car becomes "second nature" is familiar to many of us—the painstaking need at first to remember a right order for doing each movement, until this grows into a familiar routine that does not have to be thought out each time. And not only a familiar routine: the outline of the car will eventually become an extension of our personal body boundaries. The body-construct has matured, and we can now release the "thinking-out" part of our brain for the moment-to-moment control of the car in traffic. There will no longer be the need to "think out" each detail, but there will still be the need for "thoughtful movement"—thought that concerns itself with the general USE, as well as with arm and foot movements.

A new "body-construct," once learned, can be used to put oneself into a state of "thoughtful movement"; but there will always have to be a decision to switch it on. The decision has to be made, and made afresh, according to the circumstance. It may not be immediately accessible to us at a conscious level, as part of our ordinary animal awareness, but has to be directed.

Will working in this way help me to cope better with things?

Yes, but only if you are prepared to work hard at it and show considerable initiative. There are bound to be discouragements that tempt you back to your familiar pattern, and there may be a period in which you manage certain aspects of your life less effectively because of the need to develop the new pattern—just as a tennis player, cricketer, or golfer may have to relearn his technique in order to get the "bugs" out of it, and may for a time be less efficient. Indeed, working in this new way may lead at first to discomfort plus desire for change, rather than comfort plus coping better with the present. Nevertheless, conditions of physical pain may clear up fairly soon, although a temporary situation may well arise in which the pain clears up provided one works in this new unfamiliar manner, but returns when one adopts a familiar "comfortable" pattern: e.g., slumping, crossing the knees, or reacting in an overexcited manner.

Can you give me some advice about my breathing?

It is easier to detect the more subtle faults of breathing when one is lying down, but first take a look at yourself standing. Preferably remove all your clothing and stand in front of a long mirror, with your arms hanging down. Are the tips of your fingers at the same level?

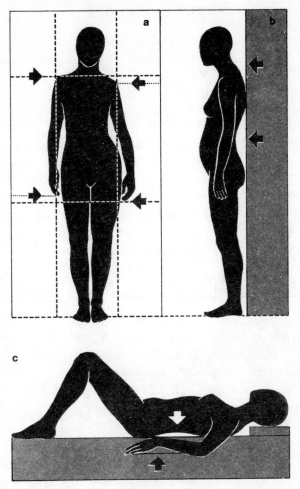

figure 25

If one hand is lower than the other, look at your shoulders. One will be lower than the other. Look at the line of your neck. It will be longer on the dropped side than on the other side.

Now imagine a perpendicular dropping from the outer edge of the lower shoulder toward the floor (Fig. 25a). It will probably fall through your thigh. Now look at the perpendicular from the other shoulder. It will probably miss the thigh by about an inch. Why?

Look at your whole chest cage. It is because your chest is displaced sideways (as in Plate 17) that your hand and shoulder are lower. This sideways displacement will affect breathing on the dropped side, and the breathing may also be further affected by a rotation of the chest backward on one side.

Now look at yourself side on (Fig. 25b). Observe the base of the neck at the back. If the neck vertebrae drop too far forward and the spine at the back of the chest is bent forward, this produces an excessive hump. The forward dropping of the neck will exert pressure on the trachea (windpipe). It is necessary to carry the head on the neck in such a way that the forward curve of the neck is corrected.

Now look at your lower back. If your back is arched, and your abdomen is protruding, your chest cage in front will usually be pushed forward, and in most people the angle between the ribs in front will be narrowed. It is difficult to get full breathing movement unless the arching of the back is corrected. This must be done in such a way as not to accentuate the hump at the base of the neck.

Lie on your back on a hard surface (Fig. 25c) with your knees pointing upward and a three-inch support under your head. Observe the bend of your elbows. The funny bone should be turned outward from the body and the inside of the elbow toward the body, so as to widen the armpit and upper arm away from the sides of the chest. If, in this position, your forearms and hands will not lie flat on the surface, your shoulder girdles are too tense and need to be released from the base of the neck.

Are you breathing? Many people, when studying or concentrating, hold their breath for long periods. Don't. When you are at rest, breathe at least ten to twelve times a minute.

Are you moving your chest and abdomen in front when you start to breathe in? Breathing in is a *back* activity. If you start breathing in by raising your upper chest in front, it is like trying to open an umbrella by pulling on the cover from the outside at the top. It can be done, but it is inefficient.

Place the backs of your hands against the sides of your chest (Fig. 26a). Imagine the gills of a fish halfway down your back on each side. Breathing in should start there, and the ribs should move out sideways against your hands. If your chest cage is displaced sideways, one side will move more than the other. Is the bottom of the rib cage nearer to your pelvis on one side than the other?

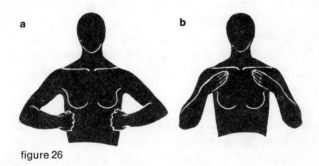

figure 26

Place your hands on the upper chest (Fig. 26b) just below the collarbone on each side, and almost touching the breastbone. When you start to breathe out, there should be a slight release of tension as the upper chest and breastbone drop. If you are very tense, a sigh will give you the feeling of the upper chest releasing.

Breathing out, at rest, should last at least twice as long as breathing in. As you finish breathing out, you will feel your stomach muscles contract slightly. In order to get the next breath into your back, you will first have to release this stomach contraction. Many breathing difficulties come from keeping the upper chest and abdominal muscles too tense in front, even at rest.

Look at your nostrils. Is one less dilated than the other? If you touch it, it will spring out slightly. Where is your tongue? At rest, it should not press on the roof of the mouth but should lie flat on the floor of the mouth. The dilated nostrils and flattened tongue will give you a better airway.

Think about your throat. When a baby screams, or when you attempt to defecate, you will notice a tightening in the throat. Some people, when they breathe in, tighten the throat region and do not release it completely when breathing out. This leads to fixation of the upper chest—an attitude often betokening fear or aggression. This tension can be removed, on breathing out, by releasing the throat and dropping the upper chest very slightly.

Look at your shoulders. The shoulder blades should never be pulled together at the back (there has been much faulty teaching about this in the past); they should lie flat on the chest cage (Plate 18).

I cannot help feeling that you think no one, in the long run, can be really happy or healthy without using the Alexander Principle. Don't you think that you have spoiled your case by saying such things as "This seems to me to be the single most important problem that medicine now has to deal with"?

The objection would certainly be valid if I had suggested that the Alexander Principle was a cure-all. But that isn't the point I am making. The recognition of the widespread presence of bacteria was not a cure-all; it simply pointed out the way in which research had to be directed. It is the same with mis-use; its manifestations need to be tabulated as carefully as were the types of bacteria. Recognition of the widespread presence of mis-use opens up a whole new field of preventive medicine, while at the same time indicating certain medical conditions—notably the rheumatic and mental disorders—in which immediate application can be made.

Indeed, it would be unhelpful to hold out something that in fact cannot be provided; or to promise great prospects to people who theoretically might be capable of working in this way, but who, when it comes down to it, will be quite incapable of it. There is so much that is clear and valuable in this approach that it would be silly to claim too much. The influence of USE on mental and physical functioning (and, therefore, on health and happiness) is quite clear; what we can never be so clear about is the extent of the trainability of people, and their willingness to use what we can teach them. However, there is in the majority of people an area, albeit small, in which their USE can be improved, with consequent improvement in their functioning (though not the "cure" of their "disease").

In the educational sphere, there is no question of overselling the Alexander Principle. The problem is to make a sufficient number of well-trained teachers available to satisfy the demand.

CHAPTER 9

Applying the Principle

... O why are we ... so fagged, so fashed, so cogged, so cumbered,
When the thing we freely forfeit is kept with fonder a care. ...
—HOPKINS, *"The Leaden Echo and the Golden Echo."*

THE MATURE REBELLION

There comes a time in most people's lives when they feel the need to take a hard look at their pattern of living. Adolescent rebellion is a rebellion against external life-forces—parents, teachers, employers, and politicians who are blamed for the difficulties and inequities that become only too clear once childhood is over. The vast impersonal world moves implacably on, and the desire for someone at least to take some notice of us, plus the desire to be rid of adult deceit and the desire not to be "gray," lead us in adolescence to upheaval and disruption. The young are living and growing, and life is to be sensed and enjoyed. They wish to be rid of the deadening junk of the past, the customs that enslave them, and the false respect that stupid people seem to demand from them.

But one can't go on blaming the older people and the outside world forever. A more mature rebellion stops saying, "The world is making me gray: they hate me without cause," and says instead, "The buck stops here with me. Just exactly what is the matter with me? Why don't I do as well as I know I can? Why does my back ache? Why is my sex a muddle? Why am I ten different people? How can I begin to take responsibility for my own problems?"

This *internal* rebellion is a request for valid principles, not for a revolution. The rebel is not necessarily a revolutionary. He is determinedly unsubdued by the pressure of external authority, but that does not lead him to a revolutionary world of terror. The rebel has no wish to exploit anyone, but simply a desire to escape from the deadening octopus of mediocrity, which tells him to be as dull as everyone else.

If he is to escape from his dullness, he needs a plan of action; he needs principles with which to escape the "system."

There is no dearth of helpful suggestions. The priest, the psychiatrist, the poet, the novelist—all have much to say about the inner life; sociologists and doctors can recommend job change, wife change, recreation change, diet change, medicine and drugs. But men and women, in the main, still lead lives of quiet desperation, in spite of two thousand years of religion, art, and science. They have periods of great humor and joy, excitement and success. By and large, though, far too many people's plans go awry, their health and happiness deteriorate, their drive peters out in frustrated boredom. They live two lives—a personal life, based on the home and family, where at least they feel real, if miserable;

and the working life, with its values of money-seeking and social status, and where they experience a quite different reality. And if they are un-unemployed, or doing a mundane job for lack of anything better, they become unreal people, in bondage to a life of tedium.

This is the lot of many apparently "normal" people. But even "normal" people will become disorganized and eventually break down when they are faced with seemingly insoluble situations. And when they are depressed and "got down" by the complexity of it all, they begin to accentuate their latent habits of mis-USE.

THE CORE STRUCTURE

I have used the phrase "core structure" to indicate the development of a personal standard of good USE, which can stop us from being "got down" and by means of which we can preserve our momentum and vitality even when external stress makes stability difficult—a core structure that will also sustain us when long periods of necessary learning have not yet given us skill and confidence.

Amid the give-and-take of personal relationship, with its "posture-swapping" and role-taking, the core structure enables us to give due respect to other people's needs and attitudes without having to copy their mis-USE. It does away with the need for the "conformity deformities" by which we are expected to show loyalty to our tribe. By giving us a capacity to maintain stability in the presence of conflict, and in the presence of unpleasant end-gainers, it also gives us a capacity to reconcile.

Most especially it helps in the moment-to-moment regulation of unwanted emotion. One of my patients expressed the help she gets from it in the following way:

Often I get a feeling of being *unsafe;* it is not an easy feeling to describe exactly, but it must date right back to childhood. The feeling is caused by other people and comes on quite suddenly. A look or a word is enough to start the feeling, which hits me in my midriff, and it makes me feel knotted up and apprehensive. Since working with you, I have discovered that physically I contract the part of my body which lies just below my ribs (this must be the region the ancients called the solar plexus), and it has the effect of making me arch the middle of my back. This seems to be the way in which I produce feelings of unsafety in myself. If I catch myself in time before this contraction sets in, the unsafe feeling only lasts for a moment. I have discovered that if I can remember to give my "orders" when I begin to get this feeling, I can stop it getting a grip. "Ordering" seems to make me able to adjust to the other person, not necessarily very well, but at least not stupidly. I can react from a secure feeling of widening across my back and shoulders, instead of from a panic feeling in my stomach. It also makes me able to often see that no reaction is called for, and that if I stay quite calm, with a feeling of being supported in my back, I can cope perfectly well with what is going on. I can see when it is appropriate to react, and when I needn't.

Feelings of safety or lack of security date from our earliest childhood, and are based on our feeling of USE. A loving, serene home atmosphere, with plenty of warm physical contact, can certainly help to make a child feel secure. Unfortunately this feeling of security usually includes also copying the parents' postures and moods and corresponding mis-use. The feeling of "right" and the feeling of security that we get from this posture may serve us well on the home ground (and many never leave the home ground), but they cannot be appropriate for other situations we must explore if we are to grow. Without a manner of USE that we can make basic to *all* situations, we are likely to feel insecure and to confine ourselves within the bounds of what we know already.

If parents know something about the principles of good USE, the child's feeling of security can be based on such good USE, and with it a loving, communicative, and non-aggressive relationship.

THE REASONABLE MAN

The patient mentioned above, with her feelings of insecurity and stomach panic, said she could prevent it happening if she "gave her orders." Just what exactly was she talking about?

The teaching and learning of a sequence of "orders" gradually come to be associated with a better resting state of balance, and with a core structure that gives a more secure balance during movement and communication. Alexander considered that by teaching people this ordering process, he was putting them, as he expressed it, "into communication with their reason," as opposed to the panic and insecurity that may come when we react by instinctive end-gaining.

Reason has had a poor press in recent years. The ways and habits of the reasonable man have been at a discount, along with the image of the "good" man. The holocaust of violence that was unleashed in World War II, plus the Damoclean nuclear bomb that was left poised above our heads, has produced an "eat, drink, and be irrational" mood —a mood of despair that our religions and our reasons should have led us to the abyss.

This has also been the half-century of the "common man." The depressed classes have become more literate and more vocal, but often not sufficiently educated to find and express their own reason. And one curious phenomenon has been a widespread acceptance of the dominant postural mood of the socially deprived classes: a posture of sullen collapse, plus an aggressive muscular contraction of the shoulders and arms—a posture that has come to be adopted by large numbers of middle-class adolescents as a way of connecting up with those for whom they have sympathy, and as an escape from the rigid strait jacket of the army and the genteel.

Caught between a Victorian ethic, which believed in reason and self-help, and a Freudian ethic, which says that reason and self-help are bound to founder on the shoals of the unconscious, modern man has had few principles that he can use intelligently. Instead he has fallen back on the ad-hoc satisfaction of his needs, as and when they arise. He relies mainly on instinct and on the habits with which he has got by in the past.

Instinct and habit have one thing in common. We react only to *one* specific aspect of the general situation that confronts us. Reason, on the other hand, implies that as many as possible of our relevant needs are taken into account before we react. Accordingly, it has seemed essential that the rational man should know as much as possible about his "relevant desires and needs." Years and years of school and university education are devoted to learning such relevant needs, so that, in theory, we can become free to work out suitable alternatives, and to set up our own "oughts" and imperatives.

But the gulf between theory and practice remains to be bridged. Reason, when learned only at this level, has proved inadequate, and this inadequacy has led, in part, to the present discontent, to the demand even for "de-schooling."

In Huxley's words:

> It is now possible to conceive of a totally new type of education, affecting the entire range of human activity, from the physiological through the intellectual, moral and practical, to the spiritual—an education which,

by teaching them proper Use, would preserve children and adults from most of the diseases and evil habits that now affect them; an education whose training would provide men and women with the psycho-physical means for behaving rationally.[23]

Reason, as taught in school and university, will always be likely to founder unless the reasoning faculty can be used in an additional way, TO DIRECT OUR DECISIONS. Alexander—and, of course, many, many people before him—realized that the reasoning, *deciding* part of our consciousness could also be employed to give directions (orders) to ourselves. But prior to Alexander, such "directing" had never been applied to USE in anything like the detail that he showed to be necessary. Indeed, it could not have been, because not enough was known about the sort of USE to which reasoning direction could be applied. Direction of USE is the missing tool that reason requires if it is not to founder on the shoals of unconscious habit.

THINKING IN ACTIVITY

The Alexander Principle has been oversimplified by some people into the need to sit up straight or to adopt an improved standing posture. These postures are an essential long-term part of the reasoning man's equipment—no more and no less—but they are only the outward visible signs of an inwardly directed tensional balance.

Let us postulate a perfect environment: a sort of scientific monastery in which the world is not too much with us; a world in which both reason and faith are considered valid (faith to let go of the known, reason to work for the unknown); a world that seeks to work by principle and not by habit.

This perfect environment is provided to some extent in an

Alexander training group, though for only a few hours a day, and not far from the customary pressures of money and family and the future. If I first describe such ideal training conditions, in which Alexander work has been fined down to its most accurate and intimate, we can then proceed to trim a little from this ideal setting to see what is possible for everyday man in everyday life.

Under such conditions—whether or not a teacher is giving personal instruction at any given moment—there will be a preoccupation with thought and movement. End-gaining (action which does not pay heed to the manner of use) is less likely to occur in such conditions, because there are none of the raucous stimuli of the bustling world to demand instant response. Subjectively, the distinction will begin to emerge between the "content" of the thought, and the actual "function" of thinking (in the sense that a car must be actually functioning before it can go from one place to another). It will be realized that there is more to thinking than manipulating ideas, whether in clear concentration or in just vague meanderings, more than doing sums, more than making sex plans, more than letters and loving and music and how to fix the furniture. There will be a growing awareness of another type of thinking, a thinking that is part of movement and stillness.

It is with this type of thinking that the Alexander student concerns himself within his training group. A state of bodily stillness is sought in which there is a personal organization of the USE perception. This personal organization ("directing") may involve a very slight muscular activity, an adjustment that is present both at rest and during action. Muscular activity, as we have seen, is never still; it may be fined down and fined down, but the gradation between stillness and activity is only one of degree. Slight oscillation is always present, even in the balanced resting state.

Under conditions of directed thinking, the student becomes increasingly aware of the muscular matrix of his decision, and of the part he can play in attending to the small shifts of muscle tension that accompany both his emotions and his insights. The appreciation of these shifts is as delicate as the finest touch of the violinist, and such directed thinking is at first a tenuous thing; any fatigue or lessening of attention can put an end to it.

We have usually taken it for granted that we can only use our minds in two deliberate ways—content-thinking (i.e., with words, sentences, music, images, etc.) and behavior control. But between content-thinking and overt behavior there is another sphere of personal life, a vast world of existence to be managed by awareness and attention (although "managed" is too forceful a term for the attentive living that is implied).

This sort of work has been going on for many years in Alexander groups. It does, however, presuppose a degree of peace and quiet that may not be easily available, except perhaps in a hospital, school, or university. For the average patient (or pupil) who embarks on a study of the Alexander Principle, detailed application to "directing" is difficult in our present economy. With increasing leisure it should be easier—and most of us are in fact far less busy than our "office hours" might imply. Certainly in the initial learning phase, it is essential to have some freedom from intrusion. Even when there are others around, most people already have a way of keeping up their own "silent soliloquy," and this soliloquy could be used occasionally more profitably in USE direction. We cannot escape from our function of being attentive human beings, except by living in a state of deadening passivity. A critical sifting process is going on, to a greater or lesser degree, in all our normal perception. Giving "direction" is like setting the focus and speed of a camera. If the focus is wrong, a blurred picture will result, which can be misinterpreted in many ways. Time spent in directing is never wasted. A far more appropriate response is possible if the focus of perception has been sharpened by directing.

THE SENSE OF REALITY

Increased self-awareness is bound to interfere with some of our social shams and to compel us to face up to reality. And most of us want reality, but when we are in a mis-used state, we may have to be taught reality. In the Alexander teaching situation, a teacher can give us a glimpse of reality through the teaching process—there is usually an opening through which a start can be made.

At first it may be only a glimpse. Many of the early learning stages will be vague, and you may have to content yourself with an intellectual confidence in the diagnosis and the procedures.

That process of slowly laying foundations may at first give only a sense of "unrealized potential," which is distasteful to many of us, and you may therefore prefer your old mis-use, however unreal it may be. The discarding of this unreal mis-use may seem like a loss at first, and loss of anything familiar is sad. You will find you are profoundly attached to your old mis-uses and the moods they maintain.

We fear new things because we fear that we may lose our familiar command of the situation. By learning a familiar command of your USE, you can acquire an abiding sense of consistency, and dispense with the need for an external familiarity. There has to be a willingness to accept the unfamiliar—a deeply implicit feeling that life is open to change.

Routines, of course, will always be needed; all sensible life is based on personally selected routines, but routines can be changed, whereas habits too easily outlive their usefulness and lead us into unreality.

The discarding of such unreality must go on. To *be* what

you can be, you have to find out what you are. *Being* what we can be means being alive, happy, and adjusted to our day-to-day life. This "all there" sense of reality is easier for children, who live in a restricted environment where their vivid sensibility allows them to "find out" all the time. Unless we, as adults, find out what we are up to with our USE —and continue to find out about our USE as things change —we will have an increasing sense of unreality.

To find out what we are is, however, only to find out the ordinariness, not the supernatural. Reality, when we find it, is ordinary and everyday—but an ordinariness in which our heightened senses can delight. It is not a question of going from the prosaic to the miraculous, but from unreality to reality.

Detailed directing—achieving a more real state through a free manner of use—is not easy for most people in everyday life; and fortunately such detail is not needed all the time. There is a difference between learning and living (although the fullest life will always be one that seeks to learn something from each thing it does). However, when we are away from the actual pressures of living—whether it be because we have broken down mentally or physically, or because we have deliberately put ourselves in a restricted learning environment—living and learning can become synonymous.

HYPNOSIS AND RELAXATION

I am often asked why I don't use hypnosis in order to help people to release their unconscious tensions. Recently a young woman suggested to me that since she was prepared to accept that her neck and chest tensions were due to some infantile trauma, might she not be able to recall the original traumatic incident if she was hypnotized? And that if she was subsequently told of this forgotten reason, might she not then more easily release the tension? A combination of pre-hypnosis and hypnosis.

The snag with all such approaches is that chest-armoring is not now one single specific mis-use, although it may have started as a specific mis-use. Over the intervening years, a most elaborate system of compensating mis-uses has been established, and the discovery of one original "trigger" cause will not now release other compensations. Indeed chest tensions could only have become so firmly established because the *general* manner of use at the original time was already disturbed. Most of us have been through many incidents of extreme fear and stress when young and if our manner of use is good we throw them off. The same thing applies to the extremes of stress which we encounter when we are adults.

There is no need to bring in hypnosis—it can only add another factor of unconscious dependence. Instead of searching for the old context, it is more useful to construct a *new* context, in the light of which the old attitude will be seen now to be insignificant.

During Alexander instruction, there will be many insights, once there is a resting state of calmer USE. In this state, almost anything can serve as a reminder of incidents or attitudes that had been forgotten.

With Alexander instruction, the old mis-use pattern is lost for a time, but it will reappear with a familiar stimulus. Against the background of a newly found awareness of better USE, it is possible to detect the abrupt transition back to the old familiar (but previously unnoticed) state of mis-use.

This insight may be extremely tenuous and may not necessarily be formulated as a clear attitude to this or that person or situation. It may take the form of a sensation, or of some new release of muscle tension, or of some new spatial awareness of how, say, the chest joins onto the lower back; or of how the pelvis can move or release in an integrated manner.

What has been said about hypnosis applies equally to "relaxation" therapy. I read in a recent treatise on relaxation that "the exercises are not difficult—in fact they are very simple." In a sense this is true. They are simple and ineffectual, except at a trivial level. How could tension habits that have been built up over many years possibly be altered by some simple rule-of-thumb procedure? There has been an alarming vogue recently among psychotherapists of trying to get their patients to relax by various forms of body contact and gentle handling. The therapist has usually picked up these techniques after a few instructional sessions from some pundit. I am not surprised that the whole subject has got a reputation for being dangerous. The technical problems of teaching a balanced resting state of USE are difficult and there cannot be a place for such simple relaxation therapy at any serious level.

It can never be a question of detecting faulty tension patterns once and for all, deconditioning them by hypnosis or relaxation, and seeing them disappear. Rather, it is a matter of continually having to refind many of them, in countless different situations, and gradually revealing the compensatory tensions that, like layers of an onion, manifest themselves when covering layers have been stripped off. Just how far the stripping should go will depend on time and inclination, and it is essential that the psychotherapist or teacher should know exactly what he is doing and how much can be tolerated.

USE must not be ignored, whatever the psychotherapeutic situation. Modern linguistics has an adage, "Don't ask for the meaning, ask for the use." The grammar of the body has to be studied in action, in living USE, not dormant in dreams or on the dissecting table. The meaning of a memory belongs with its present-moment USE. When a mis-use is reconciled back into a directive resting state, the harmful memory has gone.

The unconscious is irrelevant when we learn to live more consciously—a tautology, but the one must imply the other. Body use *is* the "unconscious" for most people. As USE becomes more conscious, the unconscious habit can lose its grip.

AN ALEXANDER LIFE-STYLE

Few people will, or can, apply the Principle without sorting out at least some of their basic living habits; and many, in time, come to value it much more for its effect on their general life-style than for its effect on their corns.

The Alexander Principle, which seeks to change habit at the very moment of reaction, is bound to have an impact on anyone who attempts it, and there have been many and varied attempts by different people to give it a style that fitted their own temperament. Huxley's "non-attachment"; Dewey's brand of pragmatism; Stafford Cripps's austere Christian Socialism; Bernard Shaw's Life Force; Ludovici's "race of mental giants"; the rationalism of a few minor rationalists; the opportunism of a score of European and American "therapists," who thought it was a bandwagon but found it was a bed of nails; the short-cutters in the world of speech training and physical education, who listened impatiently to all that talk about end-gaining; and above all, the crackpots—carnivorous, herbivorous, astrologizing, worshiping—who found a haven in Alexander's *"Nil a me alienum puto,* so long as you keep quiet and don't pull your head back." He once said to me, "If there is a crackpot within fifty miles, he will find his way to me."

It is a miracle that it survived some of this bunch, and

since in the early days anyone who was dimwitted or cross at his own learning difficulties could call it a load of rubbish, Alexander was at the mercy of malevolents, because there was no one to contradict them. It was a buyer's market for most of his life, and it is not surprising that he accepted gratefully the plaudits of any minor "authority" who was prepared to say that his work was valuable. It is also not surprising that he was distrustful of much of the human race—"lowly evolved swine" was one of his epithets in later years—and I can personally vouch that it is true he kept a blunderbuss in his room with which to scare off itinerant musicians and street criers, a splendid spectacle of Edwardian outrage.

Fortunately there has always been a hard core of common sense at the back of it all. The actual practical teaching procedures have gone on, individually and in groups, in an almost total separation from what anyone might be saying about it. (And they will continue to go on, relatively undisturbed by anything I am writing about it.)

Alexander was no saint, but he saw his Principle as a major hope for most of us. Many people have found that his Principle has opened a new door for them—not necessarily the door to wealth and success, but an escape hatch and a possible way through to what might seem an impossible personal evolution.

Fagged, fashed, cogged, cumbered, stuck in a dreary set of commitments and habits—some evolution must be attempted if a life is to be made with style and with pleasure. A very few people have over the ages chosen to explore something quite different. We have had a half-century of the common man, of the individual doing his own thing. Perhaps we can now have a half-century of the extra-vidual, the man who has not only freed himself from the compulsions of society, but who has a way of freeing himself from his own compulsions by the cultivation of an attentive resting state of USE, a way that can move him toward the life of the "whole man." Such a man, *capax universi,* will find a world of infinite charm and variety in what Alexander has to offer.

SOURCE NOTES

Chapter 2—Use and Mis-use
1. C. Sherrington, *Man on His Nature* (Cambridge University Press, 1951), p. 174.
2. W. Barlow, "Postural Deformity," *Proceedings of Royal Society of Medicine* 49 (1956): 670.
3. W. Barlow, "Rest and Pain," *Proceedings IVth International Congress of Physical Medicine, Excerpta Medica International*, series 107 (1964): 494.

Chapter 3—Balance and Rest
4. W. B. Cannon, *The Wisdom of the Body* (Kegan Paul, 1932).
5. D. Morris, *The Naked Ape* (New York: McGraw-Hill, 1968).
6. A. Keith, *British Medical Journal* 1, no. 4 (1932): 51.
7. E. Hooton, "Why Men Behave like Apes, and Vice Versa," *Science* 83 (1936): 271.
8. A. Schopenhauer, *The World as Will and Idea* (London: Kegan Paul, 1818).

9. H. Spencer, "Gracefulness," *Essays* (Williams, 1852).
10. T. Aquinas, *Summa Theologica* 1, 5.4.
11. H. J. Eysenck, *The Dimensions of the Personality* (London: Kegan Paul, 1947).

Chapter 4—Use and Disease
12. R. M. Hare, *Freedom and Reason* (Oxford University Press, 1963).
13. W. R. Gowers, "Lumbago: Its Lessons and Analogues," *British Medical Journal* 1 (1904): 117.
14. I. P. Ellman, "Fibrositis," *Annals of the Rheumatic Diseases* 3 (1942):56.
15. P. Hench, "The Management of Chronic Arthritis and Other Rheumatic Diseases Among Soldiers of the U.S. Army," *Annals of Rheumatic Diseases* V, p. 106.
16. W. Barlow, in *Modern Trends in Psychosomatic Medicine* (London: Butterworth, 1954).

Chapter 5—Mental Health
17. A. Gregg, "What Is Psychiatry?" *British Medical Journal* 5, no. 1: 101, 551 (1944).
18. H. Wolff, *Headache* (Oxford University Press, 1948), p. 102.

Chapter 6—The Psycho-Mechanics of Sex
19. Howard Gardner, "Figure and Texture in Aesthetic Perception," *British Journal of Aesthetics*, October 1972.
20. L. Corbin, *Avicenna* (London: Routledge and Kegan Paul, 1960).
21. Howard Gardner, "Figure and Texture."
22. T. Sparshott, *An Enquiry into Goodness* (University of Toronto Press, 1958).

Chapter 9—Applying the Principle
23. Aldous Huxley, "End-gaining and Means-Whereby," *Alexander Journal*, no. 4 (1965): 19.

REFERENCES

1. W. Barlow. "An Investigation into Kinaesthesia." *Medical Press Circular* 215, 60, 1946.
2. C. Sherrington. *Man on His Nature.* Cambridge University Press, 1951.
3. G. Ryle. *Collected Papers.* Hutchinson, 1971.
4. W. B. Cannon. *The Wisdom of the Body.* Kegan Paul, 1932.
5. D. Morris. *The Naked Ape.* Jonathan Cape, 1967.
6. A. Keith. "Man's Posture: Its Evolution and Disorders," *British Medical Journal* I, 451, 1923.
7. E. Hooton. "Why Men Behave like Apes and Vice Versa." *Science* 83, 271, 1936.
8. W. Le Gros Clark. *The Antecedents of Man.* Edinburgh University Press, 1959.
9. B. Campbell. *Human Evolution.* Chicago University Press, 1967.
10. A. Schopenhauer. *The World as Will and Idea.* Kegan Paul, 1818.
11. H. Spencer. "Gracefulness." In *Essays.* Williams, 1852.

12. W. Barlow. "Postural Homeostasis." *Annals of Physical Medicine* I, no. 3, 1952.

13. H. J. Eysenck. *The Dimensions of the Personality*. Routledge and Kegan Paul, 1947.

14. R. A. Granit. *The Basis of Motor Control*. Academic Press, 1970.

15. T. Roberts. *Basic Ideas in Neurophysiology*. Butterworth, 1966.

16. P. A. Merton. "Nervous Gradation of Muscular Contraction." *British Medical Bulletin* 12, 214–18, 1956.

17. D. E. Broadbent. "Introduction." *British Medical Bulletin on Cognitive Psychology*, 1971.

18. W. Barlow. "Posture and the Resting State." *Annals of Physical Medicine* vol. 2, no. 4, 1954.

19. R. M. Hare. *Freedom and Reason*. Oxford University Press, 1963.

20. W. R. Gowers. "Lumbago: Its Lessons and Analogues." *British Medical Journal* I, p. 117, 1904.

21. J. L. Halliday. "Psychological Factors in Rheumatism." *British Medical Journal* I, p. 213, 1937.

22. I. P. Ellman. "Fibrositis." *Annals of the Rheumatic Diseases* 3, p. 56, 1942.

23. P. Hench. "The Management of Chronic Arthritis and Other Rheumatic Diseases Among Soldiers of the U.S. Army." *Annals of the Rheumatic Diseases* 5, p. 106, 1946.

24. W. Barlow. "Anxiety and Muscle-Tension Pain." *British Journal of Clinical Practice* vol. 13, no. 5, p. 339, 1959.

25. H. J. Eysenck. "Dimensions of the Personality." *Op. cit.*

26. W. Barlow. *Modern Trends in Psychosomatic Medicine*, Butterworth, 1954.

27. W. Barlow. "Postural Deformity." *Proceedings of Royal Society of Medicine* vol. 49, no. 9, p. 670, 1956.

28. W. Barlow. "Anxiety and Muscle Tension." *British Journal of Physical Medicine* 10, 81, 1947.

29. A. Gregg. "What Is Psychiatry?" *British Medical Journal* V, no. 1, 551, 1944.

30. H. Wolff. *Headache*. Oxford University Press, 1948.

31. Davis, Buchwold, and Frankmann. "Autonomic and Muscular Responses and Their Relation to Simple Stimuli." *Psychological Monographs* no. 405, p. 69, 1955.
32. J. E. Goldthwaite. *Body Mechanics*. Lippincott, 1952.
33. C. Darwin. *The Expression of the Emotions in Man and Animals*. Reprinted: Thinkers Library, Watts, 1945.
34. M. Bull. "Attitude, Theory of the Emotions." *New York Nervous Disease Monograph*, 1951.
35. W. Young. *Eros Denied*. Corgi, 1967.
36. L. Corbin. *Avicenna*. Routledge and Kegan Paul, 1960.
37. H. Gardner. "Figure and Texture in Aesthetic Perception." *British Journal of Aesthetics*, 1972.
38. T. Sparshott. *An Enquiry into Goodness*. University of Toronto Press, 1958.
39. J. M. Tanner. *Growth at Adolescence*. Oxford: Blackwell, Scientific Publications, 1962.
40. W. Barlow. "Rest and Pain." *Proceedings of IVth International Congress of Physical Medicine, Exerpta Medica International*, series 107, p. 494, 1964.
41. M. Swain. "Survey of Physical Education." *Australian Journal of Physical Education*, June 1961.
42. J. Dewey. *Experience and Nature*. Open Court, 1925.
43. Aldous Huxley. *Ends and Means*. Chatto and Windus, 1937.
44. F. M. Alexander. *The Use of the Self*. Methuen, 1932.
45. G. E. Coghill. *Anatomy and the Problem of Behaviour*. Cambridge University Press, 1929.
46. Judson Herrick. *G. E. Coghill: Naturalist and Philosopher*. Chicago University Press, 1949.
47. W. Barlow. "Psychosomatic Problems in Postural Re-education." *The Lancet*, p. 659, 2 Sept. 1955.
48. Marghanita Laski. *Ecstasy*. Cresset Press, 1961.
49. D. Bannister and J. M. Mair, eds. *The Evaluation of Personality Constructs*. Academic Press, 1968.
50. Aldous Huxley. "End-gaining and Means-Whereby." *Alexander Journal*, no. 4, 19, 1965.
51. B. Pasternak. *Dr. Zhivago*. Collins, 1958.

INDEX

abdomen, 28–9
  pain in, 30, 118–19
accident-proneness, 120
adolescents, posture defects in,
    12–13, 60, 75, 134, 205
Alexander, Matthias, 4–7, 16,
    61, 102, 107–8, 120, 126,
    160, 170–1
Alexander Institute, 54
Alexander Society of Teachers,
    5
Alexander Technique, 172–3
  instruction of, 175–84
  teachers of, 54, 182–4, 199
anatomy, living, 60–3
anger and muscle tension, 129
anxiety and muscle tension,
    126–8
appendectomy, 118
Aquinas, Saint Thomas, 76

arms, 44–5
  pain in, 110
  and shoulders, 19, 41
  tension in, 127
arthritis, 20, 113–14
  of hip joint, 105–6
  see also cervical spondylosis
asthma, 116–17
athletics, 44–5, 51, 78
attitude and emotion, 131–5
"atypical facial pain," 119

back
  arching of, 32–4, 36, 39, 41,
    48, 67, 68
  lengthening of, 72, 177,
    188–9

back (*cont.*)
  overcontracted muscle in,
    86–7
  pain in, 33–4, 48–9, 60,
    72–3, 106–7, 110–12
  sideways curvature in, 49, 50
  see also spine
balance, 56–8
  of head, 70–2
  sitting, 68–9, 74–5
  upright, 63–7
  see also resting balance
behaviorism, 5, 127–8, 139
behavior therapy, 139, 173, 190
blood pressure, 104, 117–18
blood vessels, 118
"body-construct," 81, 113, 120,
    191–4
"body language," 128, 132, 134
Body Mechanics (Goldthwaite),
    130
"body wisdom," 58–60, 103–4
bowleg, 39
brain, muscle function and,
    85–6
brain chemistry, 138
breathing
  disorders, 100, 116–17
  faulty patterns of, 19, 64,
    111–12
  instructions for, 194–8
  in sexual activity, 152–4
bronchitis, chronic, 117
buttocks, tension in, 64, 67, 127

Cannon, W. B., 58
"cell assembly," 86
cervical spondylosis, 106–10
chairs, design of, 59, 73, 74
chest
  and breathing habits, 117,
    152
  expansion of, 42, 43

postural deformities in, 23,
    27–8, 29, 111, 118
  see also thorax
children
  abdominal pains in, 118
  posture deficiencies of, 12,
    54–5
  preventing mis-use in, 122,
    203–4
  sitting postures of, 30–1, 45,
    49–50, 73–4
  standing postures of, 32–3,
    50–1
Coghill, G. E., 178 *n.*
collarbones, imbalance in, 28
communication, tension during,
    128–30
"core structure," 202
coronary thrombosis, 118
cramps, 88, 119, 129, 157
Cripps, Sir Richard Stafford, 6,
    213
Critchley, Macdonald, 192

Darwin, Charles, 61, 131
depression
  case histories of, 8–9, 10
  diagnosis of, 95, 96
  and posture, 111, 132, 134
descriptive diagnosis, 94–8
Dewey, John, 171, 213
diagnosis, 92–4
  descriptive, 94–8
  prescriptive, 98–9
  and use, 100–1, 174
diseases
  diagnosis of, 94–7, 121–2
  prevention of, 99–100
  of stress, 117–20
disk
  lesion, 112
  pressure on, 87, 110
doctors, medical, 92–3

"dorsal spine," 23
drinking, 186
drugs, therapeutic, 58–9, 76,
    100, 126, 135
dystonia, 77–9, 86–90
    see also muscle tension

ears
    uneven level of, 23
    vestibular apparatus in, 70–1
elbows, 42
    and "tennis elbow," 44, 106
electromyography, 86, 102
emotion, attitude and, 131–5
emotional gusts, 186
emotional states
    and muscle tension, 126–35
    see also stress disorders
"end-gaining," 170–2, 207
    reflex, 104–5
ergonomics, 59–60, 61, 123
Eros Denied (Young), 144
"erotism," 145–6
evolution, 61–3
exercises, 115
    for breathing, 116
Expression of the Emotions
    (Darwin), 131
eyes, dropping and raising of,
    30, 71
Eysenck, H. J., 80, 117, 119

"facet block," 110
facial pain, 110, 119
fatigue, 122, 186
feedback, muscular, 80–2,
    144–5
    negative *vs.* positive, 145
feet, 39, 41
"fibrositis," 102, 110
Frank, Alma, 49

freedom, sexual, 160–3
frown, 26
"frozen pelvis," 11, 64
"frozen shoulder," 44, 106
frustration, 187

gastrointestinal disorders, 118
Gestalt psychology, 146
Goldthwaite, J. E., 130
Gowers, W. R., 102
Growth and Adolescence (Tan-
    ner), 51
gynecological conditions, 119,
    159

hands, 44, 49
    numbness in, 110
Harvey, William, 13
Head, Henry, 191
head
    balance, 70–2
    retraction of, 17–18, 20–1,
        39, 68–9, 71
    use of, 16, 19–27, 47–8, 107–
        10, 133, 152
headache, 25, 60, 66–7, 127
heart conditions, 28, 118
hip, arthritis of, 105–6
hospital care, 116, 123
hostility, muscle tension and,
    127
hump, *see* neck, hump region of
Huxley, Aldous, 5–6, 171, 205,
    213
hypertension, 117–18
    muscular, 90–1
hypnosis, 210–11

illness, *see* diseases
"inhibiting," 171–2, 176, 187

"intercostal neuralgia," 28
intestinal disorders, 118

James, William, 130, 131
jaws, 25–6
joints, arthritic, 101–2, 105,
    113

Keith, Sir Arthur, 59
knees, 39, 41, 64
    crossed, 36, 72, 77, 173
kyphosis, 106

legs, 36–41
    pain in, 106
    uneven lengths of, 29, 106
lengthening of muscle, 66–7,
    85–6
lengthening position, 72
"ligamentous strain," 110
lordosis, 33, 48, 106
love-making, *see* sexual activity
"lumbosacral strain," 110

Malleson, Joan, 159
Man's Supreme Inheritance
    (Alexander), 61
Marcus Aurelius, 76
masturbation, 161–3
medicine
    physical, 114
    preventive, 99–100
    use of Alexander Principle
        in, 122–4
    see also diagnosis
menopause, 119
mental disorders, 100, 101

causes of, 136–40
    see also emotional states;
        neurosis; stress disorders
Merton, P. A., 85
mind and muscle, 127–8, 130–1
Morris, Desmond, 59
muscle
    lengthening of, 66–7, 85–6
    and mind, 127–8, 130–1
    overcontraction of, 86–90
    physiology of, 82–6
muscle tension
    and blood pressure, 118
    and emotional states, 126–35
    in head and neck, 20, 25,
        108–9
    in jaw, 26
    relaxation of, 64, 90–1, 118,
        173, 178
    and rheumatic pain, 102,
        113
    sexual, 11, 127, 130, 156–60
    situations conducive to,
        185–7
    see also dystonia
"muscular armor," 30, 179
muscular blocks, 156–60
muscular feedback, 80–2,
    144–5
muscular texture, 146–8

Naked Ape, The (Morris), 59
neck
    evolution of, 63–4
    hump region of, 20, 30, 42,
        48–9, 63, 71, 108, 112
    overcontracted muscle in,
        66–7, 88, 127
    pain in, 9, 108, 110
    releasing tension in, 169,
        173, 175–7
    twists in, 23, 32–3, 109, 133
    use of, and head, 16, 19–25,

47–9, 107–10, 152, 175–6
nerves
  at base of neck, 20, 110
  and muscle, 82–6
neuralgia, trigeminal, 119, 120
neurosis, 117, 119, 125–7, 135
nurses, 123

objects, handling of, 186
obsessional mental states, 186
"ordering," 190–1, 203
orgasm, 149–50
orthopedics, 59
orthopedic surgery, 33–4, 111,
  115
oscillation, 79–81, 207
osteoarthritis, 105–6, 113
osteopaths, 11, 29, 110

pelvis, 36–41
  "frozen," 11, 64
  sexual movements of, 152,
    154–6
  in sitting posture, 72–3, 87
  in standing posture, 64–5
  tilted, 28–9, 36, 86
  tipped, 67
physical education, 51–3
physical medicine, 114
physicians, 92–3
physiotherapy, 114–16, 139,
  167
"pleurodynia," 28
polio, 106
"postural backache," 110
postural homeostasis, 79–80
posture
  criterion of, 75–6
  studies of, 12–13, 51–3,
    59–60
  see also sitting posture;

standing posture
"posture-swapping," 50–1, 202
premature ejaculation, 159
prescriptive diagnosis, 97–9
preventive medicine, 99–100
"primary control," 16, 49
psychiatry, brain chemistry
  and, 138
psychoanalysis, 135, 143
  see also psychotherapy
psychology, *see* behaviorism;
  Gestalt psychology
psychosomatic disorders, *see*
  stress disorders
psychotherapy, 135–6, 138,
  139, 140, 143, 212

reason, role of, 204–6
rebellion
  adolescent, 200–1
  internal, 201
reflex end-gaining, 104–5
reflexes, 61–2, 116
Reich, Wilhelm, 11, 144, 152–3
relaxation, 90–1
relaxation therapy, 173, 212–13
rest, 76, 123
resting balance, 77–82, 86–91,
  121, 207
  in sexual activity, 154
rheumatism, 101–7
rheumatoid arthritis, 113–14
rush, 187
Ryle, Gilbert, 26

"sacroiliac strain," 110
Schilder, P. F., 192
schools and colleges, posture
  problems in, 30, 51–3, 54,
  122
Schopenhauer, Arthur, 76

sciatic pain, 110
scoliosis, 23–5, 32–3, 106
Scudamore, 102
sedentary life, effects of, 42,
    45, 67
sexual activity, 142–54
    breathing in, 162–4
    and lying down, 154–6
    muscular blocks in, 156–60
    resting balance in, 154
sexual disorders, 10–11, 159–60
sexual freedom, 160–3
sexual muscle tension, 11, 127,
    130, 156–60
sexual perception, 147, 150–2
Shaw, George Bernard, 5, 213
Sherrington, Sir Charles, 18, 82
shoulders, 19, 41–3
    and back pain, 111
    "frozen," 44, 106
    pain in, 110, 133
    releasing tension in, 173, 178
sinus trouble, 121
sitting down, 17–19, 46, 68–9,
    86
sitting posture, 36–7, 45–6,
    72–5, 77
    of children, 30–1, 45, 49–50,
    73–4
    instruction for, 180–2
sleep, 76
slump, 30–1, 47–9, 72–5, 134,
    173, 186
smoking, 186
social criteria of posture, 75–6
South Africa, libel suit in, 6–7
Sparshott, T., 162
spasmodic torticollis, 119, 120
"spastic colon," 30, 118
speech, mechanisms of, 19, 64
speech therapy, 4, 7, 26
Spencer, Herbert, 76
spine, 30, 64–5, 69, 106, 111,
    119
    see also back; "dorsal spine"

squatting position, 77
stammering, 26
standing posture, 37–9, 59,
    63–7
    of children, 32–3, 50–1
    instruction for, 180–2
sterno-mastoid muscle, 25
stimulus-response psychology, 5
stomach, *see* abdomen
stress activity, muscle tension
    and, 90–1
stress disorders, 102–3, 113,
    117–20
surgery, orthopedic, 33–4, 111,
    115

talking, 186
Tanner, J. M., 51, 53
teachers of Alexander Tech-
    nique, 54, 182–4, 199
television, 46, 73–4
"tennis elbow," 44, 106
tenosynovitis, 44
tension, *see* muscle tension
texture, muscular, 146–8
thinking, directed, 206–9
thorax, displacement of, 28,
    111, 119
tics, muscular, 119
torticollis, 119, 120
trigeminal neuralgia, 119, 120
Tutin, Dorothy, 43

unconscious, 205
upright balance, 63–7
    see also standing posture
Use
    functioning and, 8–13
    meaning of, 7–8
Use of the Self, The (Alex-
    ander), 5

vaginismus, 119, 159
vertebrae, 21–3, 64, 65, 108,
110
vestibular apparatus, 70–1
voice, muscles affecting, 4, 7,
19

walking, 39–41
"wisdom of the body," 58–60,
103–4
Wolff, H., 127

Wordsworth, William, 6
wrist, 44
writer's cramp, 119, 129–30,
157

X-rays, head and neck, 21–3,
48, 108

Young, Wayland, 144

A NOTE ON THE TYPE

The text of this book was set on the Linotype in a face called Primer, designed by Rudolph Ruzicka, who was earlier responsible for the design of Fairfield and Fairfield Medium, Linotype faces whose virtues have for some time been accorded wide recognition.

The complete range of sizes of Primer was first made available in 1954, although the pilot size of 12-point was ready as early as 1951. The design of the face makes general reference to Linotype Century—a serviceable type, totally lacking in manner or frills of any kind— but brilliantly corrects its characterless quality.